LOST LOVES

Jorge Luis Borges, who knew the Valmiki Ramayana, compared its framing device to *One Thousand and One Nights* and *Don Quixote*. By seeing the Ramayana story as part of the Indian literary tradition and not merely its religious one, Arshia Sattar has performed an immensely important act of rescue. But she has done more than this. She shows how the Ramayana, at whose centre is a young couple, has all the complexity of 'a story about love'. If the story has a tragic end, dharma plays as much a role in it as do the temperaments of the two protagonists. 'I always thought I was human,' Rama says at a crucial point in the Ramayana. It is Rama and Sita's human side, their impassive public faces at war with their grieving private ones, that Sattar teases out in these compelling and erudite essays. The gods, too, she seems to be telling us, can do with a bit of empathy.

– Arvind Krishna Mehrotra

Sattar makes us realize how deeply conflicted Rama is, and therefore what a valuable guide he provides for contemporary mortals like us.

– Wendy Doniger

Arshia Sattar writes with the clinical detachment of a scholar ... and the passionate, involvement of a woman who looks 'beyond'. Her lucid commentary and provocative analyses of the Ramayana, light up Rama and Sita's extraordinary love story in a tender and wondrous way...

– Shobhaa De

LOST LOVES

EXPLORING RAMA'S ANGUISH

ARSHIA SATTAR

HarperCollins *Publishers* India

First published in India by HarperCollins in 2019
First published in India in 2011 by Penguin Books India

HarperCollins *Publishers* India, Cyber City, Building 10-A, Gurugram, Haryana-122002, India
www.harpercollins.co.in

2 4 6 8 10 9 7 5 3 1

P-ISBN: 978-93-5357-261-7
E-ISBN: 978-93-5357-262-4

Typeset in 11.5/15 Arno Pro
by Manipal Digital Systems, Manipal

Printed and bound at
Manipal Technologies Limited, Manipal

*

HarperCollins *Publishers*, Macken House, 39/40 Mayor Street Upper, Dublin 1, D01 C9W8, Ireland

For Sanjay Iyer
and
the constancy of love

CONTENTS

INTRODUCTION

My abridged translation of Valmiki's Ramayana was published at the very end of 1996. When I got the first copies, I was awed by the gravitas the work had acquired by being transformed into a heavy, black-jacketed hardback book. I put it away in my bookshelf and never really opened it until 2003, seven years later, when I had to teach the Ramayana as part of a classical Indian literatures course. Since then, in one way or another, I've been teaching from the text and around it on several occasions each year. And I have had to confront what I translated: what I put in and what I left out, what I chose to say and how I chose to say it. I have also had to consider what I might have done differently were I to do the same translation now.

In many ways, my own 'denial' of the Ramayana for all those years, between 1997 and 2003, was a reflection of what happened to many of us across the country and the world who love and work with Ramayana materials. Those were the years when the Hindu right was firmly entrenched in the national consciousness as well as in political power. This constellation of political parties, scholars, local politicians and people on the street had appropriated Rama and his story, silencing its inherent pluralism and making it the basis of their antagonism to those they perceived as hostile to Hinduism and to the Indian nation. What were we, those of us who worked with the Rama story and were of a liberal (if not always and entirely secular) bent of mind, to make of this? Was the story the Hindu right had taken as their own the same story that we were telling? Was there something in the Rama story that lent itself to this kind of exclusionary cultural and nationalistic politics? Was our hero, the righteous but troubled prince of Ayodhya, really a vengeful warrior god? These confusions made us back off from the Ramayana, to collect our thoughts and reconsider our own relationship to the text and to the story. Many of us retreated from the public sphere and the aggression of its Rama-related discourse.

Those years of silence seem to have ended. Despite the occasional incident, which reminds us that the fight for the Ramayana is far from over, the Ramayana has returned in all its pluralistic glory. Robust classical and folk performances, some mainstream and others subversive, had continued uninterrupted through these years but now there are contemporary additions to this universe, making it even richer and more diverse (for example, Ashok Banker's remarkable multi-volume recreation of the Rama story as well as Nina Paley's animated film *Sita Sings the Blues*).

It is in this context – the years of silence as well as the new flowering of 'three hundred Ramayanas' – that I have had to rethink my own Ramayana work and my relationship to the text that I translated. Were I to translate the same text now, it would probably be much the same in terms of tone and texture. The same events and conversations would be included, the same peripheral stories and lengthy descriptions of battle excluded. The difference would be that I would probably make the Epilogue, the Uttara Kanda, longer so that the English is more representative of the Sanskrit text where the last kanda is enormous. I would increase the length of that section so that readers unfamiliar with the original text would not think (as they might now) that the Uttara Kanda consists merely of Sita's banishment and its aftermath.

Because of teaching from the Ramayana and reading it over and over again in the past few years, I have developed a new intimacy with the text, one entirely different from the closeness that I had to it when I was translating. To my surprise, in this rapprochement, I find my thoughts going more and more to Rama. As a card-carrying feminist, I am shocked that it is he who draws me to him, compels me to try and *understand* his cruelty towards Sita and what it means for him to be king, perhaps even against his innermost wishes. I find myself more and more involved with Rama and I am convinced that the way to a more complete understanding of the Ramayana, especially for contemporary women, has to be through an inclusion rather than a rejection of Rama and his shocking behaviour.

The character of Rama as the ideal man and as god has captured the Indian imagination for centuries. Traditional as well as critical scholarship, whether literary or religious, has had to contend with the hero of the Ramayana in the tale's multifarious profusion in the arts and cultures of the subcontinent and beyond. The contentions have had many forms: reification, subversion, questions, dismissals, reappraisals, recreations. All of these have expanded the universe of the Ramayana almost to the point where the first extant composition of this story, that is, Valmiki's, has all but been forgotten as the trees have grown beyond the forest. Revisions and representations of the tale with its terrible beauties and its critical challenges to the enquiring mind have come from across the social, political and emotional spectrum, from marginalized communities and from the disenfranchised, from caste and class elites, from radical thinkers as well as from poets and philosophers. All of this indicates an enormous desire to 'own' the story, to make it one's own such that it speaks to one's aspirations as a class, caste, community or individual, even if those aspirations take the form of rejecting the story and its implications. In each of these cases, Valmiki's Ramayana exists as a mirage that shimmers in the distance, real but not quite, on the edge of the imagination but not fully within reach, compelling but not wholly attractive, perhaps because the seeds of what becomes dissent and discomfort lie nestled within it.

The Sanskrit Ramayana was composed sometime between 200 BCE and 200 CE and is attributed to the sage Valmiki. Over the centuries, as the story has been retold in almost all Indian languages, its characters and events have become the metaphors through which we, as Indians, understand ourselves, an alternative language which explores how we choose to live in the world. An indigenous tradition of interpretation and explanation, of developing the nuances and meanings of the Ramayana through reflection, commentary and opposition is as old as the text itself. It is these refractions and reflections that seep into the popular imagination and into popular culture – Valmiki's Ramayana, however, remains somewhat shrouded, seen and understood through the lenses and perspectives of those who are intimate with the Sanskrit epic. Many of these interpretations and retellings have been prompted by those aspects of the text that have made the tradition uncomfortable, for example, the times when Rama acts unrighteously and appears to violate dharma.

I would argue that the story of Rama cannot be ignored not because of its hero's implied perfection, but precisely because of its opposite, his inexplicable and apparently remorseless transgressions from the code, the dharma that he was born to uphold. Broadly, these transgressions are: the deceitful killing of Vali, the killing of Shambuka and his rejection of Sita. For women readers, scholars and critics, Rama's cruel mutilation of Shurpanakha would be added to this list. After Valmiki, many of the mainstream Rama stories that have been composed elevate Rama out of the realm of blame: they seal the debate on his actions by simply asserting (if not actually intervening with) the idea that Rama is blameless, his actions unfathomable to the human mind, because he is god. Rama's acts and deeds on earth are the consequence of his being an avatara of Vishnu, sent to earth to restore dharma. With this assertion of divinity coupled with dharma, it is indubitably established that Rama acts always for the good not only of his adversary/victim, but also for the good of humankind. Vali's and Shambuka's deaths (like Viradha's and Kabandha's, and even Ravana's) become their individual liberation from the cycle of birth and death that traps Hindu believers until they are rescued from it either by their own acts or by the grace of the deity they worship. Rama's rejection of Sita at the end of the war is parleyed as illusory rather than real, a way to ensure that she remains entirely chaste as well as to make it possible for the male and female divine powers to be united without hindrance. The humiliation of Shurpanakha is justified by her base nature and is an attempt to rid the world of impropriety.

As we construct Rama's multiple trajectories through the Valmiki Ramayana, the trope of memory and the loss thereof is an important one. Perhaps the most compelling idea in this universe of remembering and forgetting is the possibility of Rama's amnesia. Does Rama know he is god in the Valmiki Ramayana? And if he does, has he forgotten that? Does he need to be *reminded* of something that he knows and has temporarily (or perhaps, strategically) forgotten? Or does he need to be *told* who he is? Does he need to be introduced to the idea, after all his trials and tribulations, that he is more than those around him or does that self-knowledge need to be exhumed from the deeper reaches of his consciousness?

At the end of the Yuddha Kanda, after Sita has entered the fire, a trial of her chastity that she calls upon herself, the gods appear and ask Rama if he knows who he is, if he recognizes himself.

> Suddenly, Kubera, Yama, Indra, Varuna, Shiva and Brahma, creator of the worlds and knower of the Vedas, arrived in Lanka in their chariots that were as bright as the sun. They raised their strong arms that were adorned with jewels and addressed Rama who stood in front of them with his palms joined.
>
> 'You are the creator of the worlds and the foremost among the wise! How could you let Sita walk into the fire? Don't you know that you are the greatest among the gods?
>
> 'Long ago, you were Ritadhama, the best of the vasus. Then you were the self-born Prajapati, the creator of the three worlds. You were the eighth rudra and the fifth panchama. The ashvins are your ears, the sun and the moon are your eyes. You are visible in the time between the end and the beginning of the worlds. And yet, you have humiliated Sita as if you were an ordinary man!'
>
> Rama, the lord of the worlds, the best among those who practise dharma, said, 'I always thought I was human, that I was Rama, the son of Dasharatha. Tell me who I am. Where did I come from? Why am I here?' (Sattar, chap. 67)

Rama's bewilderment at this moment is touching, it makes him more human than at any other point in the story. Like any one of us at an intensely felt moment in our lives, Rama asks, 'Who am I and why am I here?' Of course, the answer he receives to that question is what makes him unlike all of us: he is told that he is god. Rama's demeanour after this shocking moment of revelation transcends the merely majestic, it becomes authoritative in a supra-mundane way. And it is with the understanding that he is god that Rama sallies forth into the Uttara Kanda, not simply a king who has been restored to his kingdom but a god restored to his divinity.[1]

David Shulman's poetic formulation of the profoundly existential problem at the heart of the Ramayana is articulated thus: that 'the Ramayana is a portrait of a consciousness hidden from itself' (Shulman, 93). It forces us to think about the cloud that covers Rama's knowledge of himself. Shulman's further suggestion is that Rama has forgotten that he is god and that is what makes him susceptible to human emotions and, thereby, to human failings. His amnesia is what makes him human, it makes him like us. It is, however, possible to turn things around, to re-place the magnetic north of Rama's dilemma that Shulman's compassionate compass so unerringly locates. What

---

1 The other dramatic revelation of one's true self in the Valmiki text happens to Hanuman. When the monkey search parties have reached the shore of the immense ocean that they must cross in order to find Sita, the aged bear Jambavan tells Hanuman who he is, that he is the only one with the capacity to leap the hundred yojanas that will get him to Lanka. At once, Hanuman is empowered and performs the mighty task. The Uttara Kanda, painfully aware of the problem of Hanuman's amnesia (why did this glorious monkey not know who he was and what he could do?) fills out the story of the boons that Hanuman received as a child-monkey. His mischievous antics led to him being cursed by the sages – that he would forget his special capacities until he needed them most. The curse that obscures the boons here is a reversal of the curse that obscures the boon in the case of Karna in the Mahabharata, who will forget the boon he has been given (the power to invoke the apocalyptic pashupata weapon) when he needs it most.

if Rama's amnesia is in relation to his being human, that his awareness of his divinity is constant but it is his awareness of his humanity that is obscured and troubled? What if he remembers that he is human only in flashes? Did Rama remember that he was god when he so ignobly killed Vali? Did he act as a divine instrument of a human dharma that crushes all other ways of being in the world, especially monkey ways and rakshasa ways? Or did Rama remember at this very moment that he was human and reacted as an exiled human prince desperately seeking an alliance, even at the cost of dishonour, to rescue his beloved wife?

Intrinsically attached to Rama's amnesia about his true nature, his inner self, is our amnesia as readers: what do we (choose to) forget about Rama when we think about his behaviour, his acts of injustice and cruelty, his enormous sacrifices, his unnerving equanimity? Do we forget his divinity or do we forget his humanness? And which of these choices that we make perplexes us more: Are we more disturbed that a god can act the way Rama sometimes does? Or does it truly get under our skin that a human like us can make the choices that Rama does under the most extreme circumstances?

Suppose we were to put aside the claim that Rama is god because it is a narrative dead end that closes all speculation about what might have led to these actions and what Rama might have been thinking when he performed these dishonourable deeds. As god, Rama is always right and always righteous. But if we approach him as a literary character struggling to come to terms with the hand that life has dealt him, we can try and enter his mind, try and see the events of his life as he might have seen them, and attempt to plumb the depths of his heart as he kills without justification and twice abandons the woman he loves most. The essays in this book will stay firmly located within Valmiki's composition which is the Rama story furthest from the all-encompassing bhakti universe that renders Rama's deeds unquestionable and beyond reproach.

Let us, for a moment, repeat the story of Rama at the most basic level before we enter Valmiki's complex and subtly nuanced portrait of an exiled prince who loses not only his birthright but his beloved as well. Rama is the eldest son of the wise and able King Dasharatha. He is groomed for kingship in the company of his brothers but Rama's personality, his abilities and talents further qualify him to be king. Not only will he be the rightful king when his time comes, there is no doubt that he will also be the righteous king of Ayodhya. Rama is exiled for fourteen years into the forest because of his stepmother's desire to see her own son on the throne. Bound by fate as well as by his love for his young queen, Dasharatha is unable to prevent this injustice to his elder son. In the forest, Rama, with his wife Sita and his devoted brother Lakshmana, spends time in the idyllic glades of Chitrakuta, visiting the settlements of rishis and their wives and students, learning from them how to live in the forest in order to survive. These days are spent in a peculiar mix of past predilections and the need to find appropriate ways of being in this new and unexpected circumstance. The princes are armed so that they can kill and eat animals and so that they can protect themselves and the gentle, peace-loving rishis. But they are also called upon to imitate the lives of the sages now that they have left the city and the kingdom behind. A curious blend of lifestyles emerges as the warrior princes and the delicate princess learn to live as ascetics in nature.

The presence of Rama and Lakshmana in the forest sends the local rakshasas into a frenzy of anxiety and aggression. The most significant skirmish between the princes and the rakshasas is the encounter with Shurpanakha who drags her mutilated self back to her brother Ravana with stories of Rama's prowess as a warrior and Sita's incomparable beauty. Seeking revenge and also compelled by desire for the beautiful woman, Ravana abducts Sita, leaving Rama and Lakshmana the seemingly impossible task of finding her unharmed and winning her back. As they wander through the wilderness seeking news of Sita, Rama must control his emotions as he tries to keep a clear head for the enormous task that lies ahead. Through the fortuitous alliance with the monkeys and with the special skills of Hanuman, Rama and Lakshmana assault the island fortress of Lanka and are able to kill Ravana and recover the virtuous Sita. But Rama feels that he cannot take Sita back after her long captivity in the fortress of a creature known to be both rapacious and lustful. A humiliating public trial by fire restores Sita to Rama, as her chastity and her fidelity are both endorsed by the gods. After a triumphal return to Ayodhya, Rama settles into a reign of lawfulness and goodwill.

There is no happy ending, however, as Rama's inner demons continue to haunt him. The schism between his private self and his public self, between the loving husband and the king who must be above reproach, is painfully pried open again when Rama is confronted with the citizens' gossip about his wife's time in captivity – had she remained chaste in her time away from her husband? Rama chooses to be the public man, the righteous king, and banishes his pregnant wife, for the queen cannot be under suspicion. She remains in the forest until Rama hears the story of his life from his sons and calls her back. Once again, however, he must ask her, as the woman who will, once again, be queen and the mother of his sons, to publicly prove her innocence and chastity. Sita calls upon her mother, the earth, who takes her away, leaving a heartbroken Rama to rule the land without her.

My interpretive commentary on Rama's inner torment will explore the human side of Rama and place the articulation of this conflict at the root of Sita's eloquent plea for non-violence during their exile. Were it not for her pointed criticism, readers may not have found a way to understand the demons within Rama – the demons that drove him to mutilate Shurpanakha, to slay the honourable Vali and to reject his devoted wife twice. Rama is a man torn between his own impulses towards privacy and introspection, and the aspirations and expectations of a life lived in the public realm with the dharma of delayed kingship as the paradigm within which he must act. While the genre of commentary recalls traditional Indian modes of text transmission and interpretation, this set of essays is firmly rooted in the modern quest for individual fulfilment and the creation of personal meaning in a world that seems to be spinning out of control.

Once Rama has been exiled to the forest, the disjunction between Rama's ascetic appearance and the presence of his shining weapons prompts forest dwellers to ask, 'Who are you that wear the matted locks of an ascetic and carry the weapons of a warrior?' I would like to argue that it is precisely this tension, this simultaneity of opposing symbols that Rama carries within and without, that define his inner conflict. Rama comes to the forest as a divested prince, with the lives and the aspirations of the sacred forest dwellers as his models. His father has been disgraced by lust in his dotage, letting his desire to please his young wife override his duty as a king and to his eldest son. These actions, apart from embarrassing Rama, have also thrown his life into disarray. Rama seeks the quiet, meditative life of the forest to come to terms with all that has happened to him and all that he must become in the future.

But that is not to be. He is required to behave as a prince in exile, a man waiting to be a king, a kshatriya in abeyance whose dharma as a warrior, nonetheless, must guide his actions. At the same time, Rama is determined to not display the same weakness (a shameful attachment to women) as his father – this shadows all his relationships with women and impinges particularly on his life with his own wife Sita. All the more reason that he finds the life of the forest-dwelling ascetics attractive – they have renounced their conjugal obligations and live with their wives as companions, rather than as sexual partners. Even as Rama and Sita settle into the gentle idyll of the forest, Sita is kidnapped and Rama is catapulted, once again, into his role as a warrior prince who must rescue his wife and restore the honour of his clan. Even when he wins her back, his own conception of the chasm between his public image and his private desires torments him and causes him to make further sacrifices.

The story of the Ramayana is a story of trial and tribulation, of the subtlety of right and wrong, of love and loss. The

Ramayana tradition has remained vital and vibrant for precisely this reason: that we continue to debate the righteousness of Rama's actions and that we continue to seek answers that are meaningful to us, in our time and space, for what this man, exemplar of a culture, chose to do. What has perplexed readers and writers of the Rama story over the millennia is Rama's apparent coldness, his increasing detachment from Sita (whom he loves to distraction as witnessed by his overwhelming despair when he loses her), his determination to remain publicly unimpeachable and his unwavering commitment to the inhuman demands of his father. I suggest here a cartography which will allow the contemporary reader to see Rama and Sita as compelling characters within a complex literary mosaic, a map by which the twenty-first-century individual can understand these characters as living, breathing humans, shorn of the religious and spiritual significance in which a growing tradition has confined, and necessarily restricted, them. By relocating Rama and Sita in a literary rather than a religious universe, I hope to make their existential conflicts and resolutions newly accessible and inspiring.

THE ABSENCE OF THE PAST

DOES RAMA KNOW HE IS GOD?

The essays in this book, all of which are intended to be read as separate pieces, are predicated on the fact that Rama acts as a human hero for most of his life as Valmiki tells it in the Ramayana.[2] This opening essay will try and establish a framework within which the following essays can be considered and introduce the ideas that are developed more fully in the other essays.

David Shulman's remarkable phrase that Rama is 'the portrait of a consciousness hidden from itself' (Shulman, 93) provides the perfect entry point for a deeper understanding of this complex hero whose life seems to have spun out of control. Of course, Rama is an epic hero whose trials and triumphs conform to the tropes and structures of the genre in which he appears: he is a warrior who has to engage a formidable enemy in battle, he has to leave his homeland on a long journey that brings him back a changed man, he travels through parts unknown and seeks the aid of beings unlike himself to

[2] Throughout this book, the Ramayana refers specifically to Valmiki's Sanskrit poem. All other tellings of Rama's story will be referred to by their given names or by the names of their composers; for example, the Tamil story might be called the Kamba Ramayana and the Hindi text the *Ramcharitmanas*.

accomplish his goals. And through all of this, the hero has the special favour of the gods.

Because Rama is a hero whose story is told within a world of Hindu ideas, aspirations and constraints, his heroic tale is coloured not simply by the particular favour of Hindu gods, but bound by crucial and culturally specific referents. The hero's battle with destiny is common to all epics, but the Ramayana and the Mahabharata further burden the quests of their heroes with boons and curses, karma and dharma. And, placing an even greater demand on the actions of the heroes, the Hindu epics layer their heroes with their own divinity. In the Mahabharata, Krishna knows he is god and reveals himself as such when the occasion demands it. In Valmiki's tale of Rama, the question remains as to whether Rama knows he is god at all: Does he know that he is god all the time? Do flashes of his own divinity come upon him only at crucial moments? Does he know he is god only when others around him act as if he has the power to liberate them from their lives or situations? Or does he recognize himself as divine only when he is told who he is and when he listens to the story of his own life?

The Bala Kanda weaves a long and complex story around the birth of Rama and his brothers who are engendered from a gift of food proffered by a divine being that emerges out of the sacrifice that Dasharatha is performing for the birth of sons. The food ensures that Dasharatha's queens will produce sons who are avataras and amshas of Vishnu, born on earth to vanquish the mighty rakshasa Ravana. Here, the issue of Rama's divinity is beyond question as it is clearly stated, but how this divinity will be manifest and how it will be made known to

Rama and those around him remains open to storytelling, if not to theological debate.

The argument could be made that there are two Ramayanas within the composition that is attributed to Valmiki – one which consists of the five middle books and the other which includes the Bala Kanda and the Uttara Kanda as integral parts of the story.[3] It is also in these outer books that Valmiki himself appears as a character and a narrator of the great tale. We can reasonably suggest that the two Ramayanas tell two stories that differ on the crucial fact of Rama's divinity and his own knowledge of it. In the story of the middle books, Rama seems not to know that he is god until the end of the war when the other gods descend to redeem Sita and tell Rama that he is Vishnu. In the story that includes the outer books, the Bala Kanda and the Uttara Kanda, the audience knows that Rama is god and it would appear that Rama knows it as well. This critical difference allows us to approach and understand the character of Rama and the nature of his deeds in very distinct ways.

In the story of Rama that is bracketed by the Bala Kanda and the Uttara Kanda, there is nothing to suggest that Rama knows he is god. In fact, it is quite to the contrary: the story opens in the Ayodhya Kanda with Dasharatha considering abdication in

---

3 There is consensus among scholars about the fact that the first and last books of what now constitutes Valmiki's 'text' – the Bala Kanda and the Uttara Kanda – were composed later than the five middle books: Ayodhya Kanda, Aranya Kanda, Kishkindha Kanda, Sundara Kanda and Yuddha/Lanka Kanda. There is, however, still much that might be said about how this affects the story of the Ramayana and the character of Rama in particular.

favour of his eldest son Rama who is 'born from his flesh' (Sattar, chap. 13) and at the end of the Yuddha Kanda, the gods appear after the war with the rakshasas and tell Rama that he is Vishnu when they return Sita to him. Until that point, Rama is simply an exceptional man among men. It is almost as if the return of Sita and the proof of her chastity are what Rama needs for his divinity to be realized by himself as well as by those around him. After this dramatic revelation, Rama and Sita return to Ayodhya and Rama reclaims the kingdom.

In the story of the five middle books, the fact that Rama is declared to be god at the end of the war with the rakshasas allows us to review his acts and, as we choose to examine them retrospectively in the light of his divinity, they appear transformed. The killings of Viradha and Kabandha have already been depicted as moments of liberation for the cursed creatures. But now, if Rama is divine and has a purpose on earth, we can see the mutilation of Shurpanakha as the catalyst that brings Ravana forth as he must be drawn into battle and killed for the good of the three worlds. The killing of Vali becomes another moment of divine grace where the victim is freed from the cycle of rebirth and redeath, and the rejection of Sita after the war becomes a means for the public revelation of Rama's divinity.

However, if in the story told between the Ayodhya Kanda and the Yuddha Kanda, we take Rama to be a man struggling to overcome the obstacles in his path and in his heart, then we would be justified in seeking explanations for why he does the things he does and why he does them in the way he does. I argue elsewhere that Rama is deeply troubled by two things: his embarrassment at his father's attachment to his young queen, and his disappointment with himself at not being able to fully live out the ascetic code which he had found so compelling during his forest exile. His discomfort with himself causes him to act or react unfairly in certain situations.

When Shurpanakha finds Rama, Lakshmana and Sita in the forests of Dandaka, she is utterly captivated by Rama's good looks and says to him, 'I am in love with your good looks, Rama. I think you must be the best of men. Be my husband and stay with me for a long time!' (Sattar, chap. 29). Rama begins to tease her, pointing her to his handsome brother who has no wife with him. But when Shurpanakha attacks Sita, it is Lakshmana who cuts off her nose and ears in imitation of his brother's earlier mutilation of Tataka.[4] In that encounter, Vishvamitra had urged Rama not to hesitate to kill Tataka simply because she was a woman. Rama uses his own judgement at the crucial moment and says to Lakshmana, 'I will not kill her because she is a woman. But I will destroy her strength and her ability to move' (Sattar, chap. 6). But the danger to his life finally persuades him to release one of his mighty arrows and kill her.

---

4 There are other texts and versions of this incident where Shurpanakha's breasts are cut off along with her ears and nose. This makes the mutilation explicit as a more obvious, if infinitely more cruel, punishment for the sexual advances that Shurpanakha had made to the brothers. Further, Shurpanakha is not killed by the brothers, but the breasts that make her who she is, a woman, are cut off. This replicates what had happened with Tataka, where Rama says that he will not kill, but he will destroy her power to move. The power to travel through air and water and through the earth was the very thing that made Tataka who she was.

Rama's agitation at Shurpanakha's unbridled sexuality could well be the result of his resentment towards his stepmother Kaikeyi whose sexual favours had kept Dasharatha in such thrall that he was unable to prevent Rama's banishment from the kingdom. Rama has no doubt that Kaikeyi had taken full advantage of the ageing king's attachment to her to ensure that her son became king. On the few occasions when Rama laments what has happened to him, he mentions Kaikeyi as well as the king's inability to control his passion, a sentiment echoed by Lakshmana and others. Rama's displaced anger finds its object in the person of the besotted rakshasi and, ironically, triggers the events that lead to Sita being abducted.

The long period of separation from Sita also feeds Rama's anxiety about women and their sexuality. His greater concern is for his wife's chastity rather than her physical safety in the time that they are apart. In a masterfully orchestrated public event, Rama rejects Sita, saying that he cannot take back a woman who has lived in the house of another man for such an extended period of time. Clearly, what Rama fears most is gossip that will liken him to his father, a man so in love with his wife that he was willing to face scandal for her sake.

Sita's humiliation causes her to ask for a trial by fire to prove that she has remained faithful to her husband through her captivity. For Rama, the issue is not resolved with the gods' vindication of Sita and the public acceptance of her chastity. When they are back in Ayodhya and Sita is pregnant, gossip surfaces about her time with Ravana and Rama finds himself unable to let her stay in the city as his queen and the mother of his heirs. What Rama had fearfully imagined at the end of the war – market gossip about Sita – has actually come to pass. Rama fails to stand by her, by his earlier decision to take her back with confidence and even by the word of the gods. He sends her into the forest where she gives birth to their twin sons. Years later, when Rama recognizes his sons at his sacrifice as they recite the story of his life, he calls Sita back. With very little hesitation, he asks her again, in front of their sons and the kings and commoners gathered there, to prove that she has been faithful to him all her life.

In the incident with Shurpanakha and in his conduct towards Sita, Rama has acted through his unresolved feelings about his father's last decree. All those years ago, he had been able to use the dharma of obedience to his father's wishes as the impetus to renounce the kingdom and go into exile. But as time has gone by, we see that the emotional wound Rama carries from that life-changing moment is far from healed. Not only does his resentment manifest itself in his actions, he also seems to grow more and more anxious about the implications and consequences of women's sexual desire. Further, since it was Dasharatha's attachment to Kaikeyi that led to his grave error, Rama realizes at the very outset that it is attachment itself that he has to transcend. He renounces his conventional ties – to the kingdom and to his family – as he leaves for the forest, understanding, perhaps, that it is attachment which clouds judgement when hard choices have to be made and unpleasant decisions taken.

It is the virtue of non-attachment that attracts Rama to the way ascetics lead their lives away from the city and from the world at large. The anguish that Rama feels when he has to reject Sita after the war and then again when she is pregnant makes him realize that, for all his efforts, he has not been able to overcome his love for her. In order to prove to himself and to others that he has managed to contain that love, Rama is harsher to Sita than he needs to be. Rama's disappointment at his own lack of detachment and his fear of being judged to be like his father collide in his treatment of Sita, making him more cruel towards her than he might otherwise have been, were he not so internally troubled.

How do we explain Rama's killing of Vali, if he is a man and not a god? It is clear that there is a spontaneous sympathy between Rama and Sugriva when they meet – both are in exile and both have been deprived of their wives and their kingdoms. In Rama's case, there can be no doubt that these deprivations have been unjust, but there cannot be as much clarity about Sugriva's situation. Though Vali may well have been the more worthy ally (braver, a better warrior and a more noble king), circumstance makes Sugriva Rama's ally in the search for Sita and the impending war with the rakshasas.

Rama has to be aware of how tenuous Sugriva's claims to the throne of Kishkindha are – he is the younger brother and he placed himself on the throne when Vali was missing, presumed dead. Neither of these situations – that is, as the younger brother or as the ostensible regent rather than as the obvious successor – gives Sugriva an inalienable right to be king. Rama has just come from a situation where his younger brother legitimately (if unjustly) can occupy the throne. Bharata refuses, and is finally persuaded to rule in his brother's name until Rama returns. Rama is also painfully conscious of how court intrigue can work and although he trusts Bharata completely, he knows that the human heart can be swayed and that power is compelling.

Rama throws his lot in with Sugriva partly because of sympathy and partly because he sees the bloody dispute over the throne of Kishkindha and the bitter enmity between the brothers as one version of the situation that he himself is in. What if Bharata chose to stay on the throne after Rama's return? What would Rama's options be at that point – more years in exile or a fratricidal war?[5] Given Rama's anxiety about his wife as a captive in the palace of another mighty monarch, surely he must have thought of what might have happened if he had left Sita in Ayodhya under Bharata's care. Rama sees that Vali has taken over Sugriva's wife when he reclaims the kingdom for himself. The thought that Sita might have been in a similar situation had she stayed in Ayodhya must make Rama even more concerned about her abduction and her prolonged captivity. When he rejects Sita after the war, he says, 'Go to Lakshmana or Bharata or to anyone else who pleases you!' (Sattar, chap. 67) inadvertently expressing this anxiety about his brothers and their relationship with Sita.

---

[5] The Ramayana acts as an idealized mirror to the way issues of dharma and kingship are handled in the Mahabharata. Rama and Bharata will do all that they can to avoid a fratricidal war unlike the cousins in the Mahabharata who are also involved in a dispute about rightful kingship. So also, Sita's humiliation after the war, where she is called out into public and renounced by her husband, can be seen as a milder version of Draupadi being dragged out, menstruating, in front of the men in the Kaurava court.

Once again, Rama is unable to place his personal circumstance aside and judge a situation objectively. All his anxieties explode when he sees Vali enjoying the pleasures of the kingdom in the fullest sense of the word. Despite the fact that the monkeys of Kishkindha live by a different set of social mores, a dharma that is not the kshatriya dharma that Rama has to uphold, Rama kills Vali for taking his brother's wife and for reclaiming the kingdom that was rightfully his – both are actions that he fears in his own life. The fact that Sugriva takes Tara, Vali's wife, after Vali is killed does not excite the same rage in Rama. Rama pragmatically chooses to ignore Sugriva's transgressions and his somewhat unstable temperament, forgiving him for the very same violations for which he had killed Vali, because he needs him as an ally.

However, if Rama is human, his dastardly killing of Vali can be attributed to emotion rather than reason. Rama had no personal enmity with Vali, Vali was engaged in combat with Sugriva when Rama shot him, and, worst of all, Rama was hidden from view and shot Vali in the back. Rama's pact with Sugriva, another emotional rather than rational choice, is what makes it necessary to kill Vali. The human Rama of the middle books of the Valmiki Ramayana proves to be like us: tormented, anxious, confused and, quite often, wrong in what he does. What draws us to his failures is that he has striven so hard to rise above himself and above common human failings. Rama's inability to fulfil his personal aspirations, at such terrible cost to himself and to others, remains compelling if we see him as someone trying desperately to keep his head above water as the currents swirl around him and pull him off course.

The divine Rama of the Ramayana (and the later Ramayana tradition which includes all the Rama stories that come after Valmiki's) is far less problematic simply because Rama's divinity makes all his actions ultimately right and righteous. While this is a neat explanation, it is problematic as it places Rama as paradigm for human behaviour out of reach since all his righteousness emerges from the divine in him rather than from the exceptional human in him.

Moreover, a divine notion of what is right can appear incomprehensible to the (limited) human mind[6] and, therefore, Rama's divine actions as a model for human behaviour continue to generate debate. While it is easy to see his obedience to his father's befuddled wishes as paradigmatic in terms of how human sons should respect the wishes of their fathers, Rama's killing of Vali and his treatment of his wife are harder to understand, even as acts of a god. And it is here that the arguments over Rama and his righteousness ultimately get located. Would/Should a god have killed Vali in such a cowardly fashion? Or demanded proofs of Sita's chastity with such metronomic regularity?

---

[6] This is much like Krishna's deeds and his understanding of what the world needs in the Mahabharata, where his manipulation and machinations before and during the war leave us with more questions, about his character and the nature of a god who acts in the world, than answers. The Hindu epics play with the idea that the gods act on earth in ways that cannot be immediately understood as being righteous, but they also demand that the audience for these stories believe that these actions are ultimately justified for the protection of dharma.

David Shulman parses his inspired insight that Rama's life is a portrait of a consciousness hidden from itself to say that Rama only has flashes of his own divinity, that it is not a constant state of knowledge and being in which he exists. These moments of truth are unpredictable and electric, like lightning that illuminates a landscape so briefly that the shadow falls even before the flash is over. The shadow that falls is amnesia and the cataclysmic experience of the truth is forgotten even as it is understood.[7]

What if we were to reverse Shulman's idea and argue that these razor-sharp flashes of intuition which rip through the shroud of Rama's amnesia reveal to Rama his human rather than his divine nature? What if Rama knows that he is divine, in the main, and has moments of jagged clarity when he realizes that he is human as well? By this argument, we could say that it is when he remembers that he is human that he rejects Sita, knowing that a human Rama would have doubts about her fidelity, that he would succumb to an anger provoked by an irrational sexual jealousy. Moreover, a human Rama would

---

7 The trope of being allowed to forget a vision of god is common in the mythology of Krishna. As a child, when he allows his mother Yashodhara to see the universe in his mouth, he also lets her forget what she has seen so that she can treat him as her naughty little boy all over again. Similarly, when he displays his awesome and terrifying universal form to Arjuna in Kurukshetra, Arjuna too is allowed to forget what he has seen and continue into battle with simply his special friend as his charioteer. Rama forgetting himself is somewhat different, but the idea that divinity can be revealed and forgotten remains interesting both narratively and theologically.

carry the scars of Dasharatha's folly, unable to forget that it was a desirable and desired woman that had been the cause of his own trials and of his father's loss of reputation. The human side of Rama surfaces again in his encounter with Vali where he kills the monkey because he cannot vanquish the demons in his own mind, demons that point to more realistic scenarios involving brothers and disputed thrones and wives abandoned in royal apartments. In Rama's idealized, divinely controlled world, there are no internecine battles and no fraternal blood is shed when kingship is snatched from one brother by another. Similarly, kings do not covet their sisters-in-law and regents rule from outside the palace in symbolic and sympathetic exile. Rama's unexpected tears and anger are also his human side remembered, recalled and grasped tightly for the precious few moments when the present can be lived fully and completely, rather than through a split human–divine consciousness.

The Ramayana as a whole would encourage us to believe that these contradictory and oppositional ways of being in the world – that is, as human and as divine – exist simultaneously in Rama's person. Holding to that position, we can reasonably explain Rama's more elevated deeds as manifestations of the divinity in him and his more contentious acts (like the killing of Vali and abandoning Sita) as human. Arguing that Rama has to remember that he is human brings him within our reach because he behaves as humans might and often do, impelled by doubts, insecurities and fears as much as he is by love, loyalty and courage. But it would seem to militate against his function as a paradigm for behaviour because his human moments are the ones when his thoughts and actions are the least worthy of imitation. Nonetheless, Rama's continued significance lies not in the perfection that tradition has thrust upon him, but in his failure to rise above human emotions and weaknesses. A god who can forget his divinity in order to show us the enormously tragic consequences of our frailties is surely far more compelling than one who remains unreachable in his distant righteousness and perfection. It is precisely in his failure that we learn, it is in his crushing personal defeats that we understand the meaning of our lives. If we see Rama as one of us, the Ramayana becomes more poignantly a story that explores the human condition rather than one that stridently declares the unimpeachable nature of divinity.

THE PRESENCE OF THE PAST

RAMA'S REACTIONS TO HIS FATHER'S ACTIONS

The transition from crown prince to beloved king is not smooth for Rama, who has to wait fourteen long and trying years before he can take his rightful place on the throne. Fate intervenes in Rama's perfect young life in the form of Dasharatha's favourite wife, Kaikeyi, who allows herself to be persuaded that it is her son who should be king. Rama's immediate future is turned upside down by Kaikeyi's wilfulness, but it is his father's past and his father's fate that transforms the queen's outrageous demands into a bitter reality for Rama. Not only had Dasharatha promised Kaikeyi two boons when she saved his life in a long-ago battle, he is also carrying the curse of an old couple whose young son he had mistakenly killed. The old couple's curse ensures that, like them, Dasharatha too will be deprived of his beloved son in his old age, and will die without him by his side. In a narrative universe where the past is always present (through karma, boons and curses), it is possible to see Prince Rama's fate as determined not by his own actions but entirely by his father's past – curses and boons given to and by Dasharatha are what allow Kaikeyi's wishes to be fulfilled. In a classic case of overdetermination, Dasharatha is bound by more than one karmic fetter that forces him to give in to Kaikeyi's demands and exile his son. Rama, on the other hand, can be seen as a victim of circumstance, paying an extremely high price for his father's follies. Moreover, Rama's reactions to his father's actions also have an enormous impact on his life when he becomes king.

Dasharatha is besotted with his young and lovely wife Kaikeyi: he will do everything in his power to please her, even at the cost of his reputation within the palace, among his other wives and even among his subjects. When Kaikeyi retires to her 'anger' chamber so that she can manipulate the king into banishing Rama and crowning Bharata in his place, an agitated Dasharatha rushes to her side.

> The lovelorn king spoke anxiously. 'Has someone been rude to you or spoken to you harshly? ... Is there anything I can do to make you happy? Would you like an innocent man punished? Or a guilty man set free? I will do anything you like, even give up my life! ... You know how much I love you ... I swear by all the merit I have earned for my good deeds that I shall do whatever you ask!' (Sattar, chap. 15)

The poignancy of the great king bartering his virtue for a kind word from his queen is heightened when Kaikeyi unveils her plan and refuses to budge.

> The great king, protector of the earth, wept like a man who has lost everything. He was so enslaved by this woman that he fell at her feet. But she moved away so that he could not touch them.

> The mighty king lay on the floor, a place wholly unsuited to him. (Sattar, chap. 15)

Dasharatha is stunned into silence when he realizes that he is honour-bound to let Kaikeyi have her way. It is the confident young queen who conveys the news of the banishment to her righteous stepson. Over and over again, Rama says that he will obey his father's wishes and that it is without sadness that he goes to the forest. Rama says to Kaikeyi, 'You know I do not crave wealth nor material things, that I am like a rishi in my devotion to dharma. I would do anything to please my father. There is no greater dharma than service to one's father and obedience to his wishes' (Sattar, chap. 15).

The bulk of Valmiki's Ramayana establishes the fact that Rama obeyed his father's wishes with remarkable grace and dignity. Not only did he redeem his father's pledge, he even forswore hostility towards Kaikeyi and her son Bharata. His preternatural calm and serene acceptance of this sudden catastrophe in his life is brought into sharper relief by the reactions of those around him: by his mother Kaushalya's grief, his brother Lakshmana's rage, and the bewilderment of the palace retainers and courtiers. Kaushalya rails against the unfairness of it all and Lakshmana rants against his father's senility. He urges Rama to take the law and dharma into his own hands and overthrow the aged monarch, who is surely no longer fit to rule the great kingdom. Rama admonishes them both and finds solace in his wife Sita, who does not question the king's command even as she begs to accompany her exiled husband into the forest.

While Rama hides his personal discomfiture by expressing concern about the effect the news will have on others, there are enough indications that he has been shocked and hurt by what has just happened.

> Though Rama had renounced the kingdom and decided to live in the forest, his mind was calm, as though he had transcended the world. Collecting himself, he suppressed his grief as he went into his own apartments to tell his mother the unhappy news. He entered the palace where everyone was celebrating, but he disguised his emotions so that the ones that he loved most would suspect nothing. (Sattar, chap. 15)

It is only in front of Sita that his face shows how hard the news of his banishment has hit him. He goes to tell her and 'he seemed sad and careworn, his face beaded with sweat' (Sattar, chap. 17).

Rama maintains his composure when he is told of his banishment, but when he tells Lakshmana what has transpired, Lakshmana loses his temper and urges Rama to overthrow the king.

> As Kaushalya wept, Lakshmana spoke, his words appropriate to the situation. 'Mother, I, too, do not like the fact that Rama has to give up the kingdom and go into the forest because of a woman's whim! The king is old and senile and succumbs to his lust. Who knows what he might say in the throes of passion! ... I shall kill my father who is impotent and

> infatuated with Kaikeyi! His dotage beckons but he frolics like a youth!' (Sattar, chap. 16)

Rama's response to Lakshmana's bitter rage is righteous and he cites other sons in the Ikshvaku clan who have obeyed their fathers' unreasonable wishes.

> 'Obeying a father's command is the highest dharma of all … I cannot disobey my father simply because Kaikeyi, our mother, asked him to command me thus. Give up your ignoble ideas inspired by the duties of a kshatriya! Follow my example. Take refuge in dharma and not in violence.' (Sattar, chap. 16)

In the forest, however, Rama echoes Lakshmana's words and harsh judgement, admitting that his father had succumbed to infatuation (if not lust) and has wronged his eldest and most obedient son. Away from his role as the crown prince, Rama is able to shed his public posture and allow himself a moment of self-pity and anguish. On their first night away from the city, after Lakshmana has made sure that they are all comfortable, he sits with Rama by the fire as they contemplate their bleak and uncertain future in the forest. Rama begins by grieving for his father, who must surely be in anguish without his beloved son.

> Rama, who deserved the best of beds, lay down on the bare earth and continued talking sadly … 'When I think of the disaster that has befallen me as a result of the king's infatuation, I feel that the pursuit of pleasure must be even

> more compelling than the pursuit of wealth or dharma. Even an ignorant man would not renounce his son for the sake of a beautiful woman. But our father has abandoned me, his most obedient son!
>
> 'Ah! Bharata is so fortunate! He is happy with his wife by his side, enjoying the pleasures of ruling over Kosala. He alone enjoys the pleasures, since my father is too old and I am stuck in the forest! He who abandons wealth and dharma and chases after pleasure shall soon destroy himself, like Dasharatha did.' ... Rama wept in his sorrow and then spent the rest of the night in silence in that lonely forest. When his tears had spent themselves as a forest fire dies down or an ocean calms itself after a storm, Lakshmana consoled his brother. (Sattar, chap. 21)

This is Rama's first verbalized criticism of his father, the wise and noble Dasharatha, a criticism that will be repeated later in the story, but always and only to Lakshmana. To begin with, Rama speaks of his unexpected exile as a 'disaster', suggesting that for all of his public equanimity, he has been shaken by this sudden turn of events. He even allows himself a moment of envy for Bharata who is enjoying the pleasures of the kingdom while he himself is 'stuck in the forest'. Also telling is Rama's backhanded swipe at Dasharatha, who cannot enjoy the pleasures of the kingdom because he is 'too old'. Implied here is a certain repulsion: too old to enjoy the pleasures of a kingdom, but clinging to desire for a young woman. Rama's assertion that he does not value wealth is repeated often in the forest years, and it develops slowly into a hierarchy of values where wealth and pleasure are placed below the pursuit of dharma. Even more so, the pursuit of comfort and pleasure become the basis of Rama's criticism of his father, they become the wellspring of his anger at the fact that even a great monarch, in the twilight of his good life, could choose creature comforts and bodily pleasures over the right and the good.

It is reassuring to know that Rama is troubled by his change of fortune. One could expect anger at the injustice, or even at the simple twist of fate, that has turned him from a man who was to be king to a homeless wanderer in the forest. Lakshmana's anger on his brother's behalf makes us sympathetic to both men. But it is Rama's tears that move us: he weeps not from rage but from hurt. This is among the first glimpses we have of Rama's inner life and it reminds us that, for all of his public perfection, Rama is troubled and has to find the strength to deal with the extraordinary hand that fate has dealt him.

Rama is not simply hurt by his father, he is also deeply embarrassed by what has happened. He is aware that Dasharatha's magnificent reputation as a good and just king, an upholder of dharma, built painstakingly over sixty thousand years, has been destroyed by this single act of choosing (however overdetermined that 'choice' might have been) to submit to his young queen's ambitions for her own son. Rama knows that Dasharatha will no longer be remembered for the righteousness of his reign, but for this one irredeemable act of injustice against his son. Dasharatha's fall from public grace because of an uncontrollable desire for his wife will haunt Rama through his years in the forest and will, ultimately, affect his relationship with Sita.[8] Somewhere along the way, deep inside himself, Rama decides that under no circumstances whatsoever would anyone ever be able to say that he acted like his father – that when he, Rama, was faced with a choice that involved public dharma and personal relationships he, too, failed to do the right thing because of his love for a woman.

The consequences of this decision become shockingly clear when Sita is rescued after the war with the rakshasas. Ravana has been slain by Rama and Vibhishana is now king of Lanka. The monkeys rejoice on the battlefield and the defeated rakshasas pledge their allegiance to their new king. Sita hears the news of her husband's victory from Hanuman in the ashoka vana where she has been imprisoned for what seems to her an interminable period of separation from her beloved. She is anxious to see Rama again and tells Hanuman so. Hanuman takes this message back to Rama who is still on the battlefield. Contrary to all expectations, Rama does not rush to meet her.

---

8 In this matter, Rama's mortification most resembles that of Hamlet, who also could not get over the unbridled sexuality and lust for power in his parents' generation. The passions of their parents place Rama and Hamlet in a similar situation in that neither can inherit the throne that is rightfully theirs. Also, as Hamlet vents his frustration and anger against women on Ophelia, so too, Rama's public attitude towards his beloved, Sita, is profoundly affected by what happened in his father's private chambers. One might argue that Hamlet's anguish is deeper because of the incestuous element in Gertrude's marriage to her erstwhile brother-in-law Claudius, but one might equally imagine that, within a Hindu universe where Rama is propelled towards public and private righteousness, Dasharatha's failure in both realms affected Rama and his subsequent actions deeply.

> Rama was silent for a moment and his eyes filled with tears. He sighed and looked down at the ground and then said to Hanuman, 'Let Sita bathe and wash her hair. Let her adorn herself with jewels and anoint her body with rare unguents. Then bring her here as soon as you can!' (Sattar, chap. 67)

Vibhishana makes sure that Sita has all that she needs to make herself worthy of an appearance in public and leads her out. 'Rama seemed preoccupied and deep in thought, even though he knew that Sita, who had spent so many months in the home of the rakshasa, had come. Joy, depression and anger flooded over him' (Sattar, chap. 67). Instead of greeting his beloved wife, Rama turns his anger on to Vibhishana and berates him for trying to control the surging crowds of monkeys and rakshasas, all eager for a glimpse of the woman for whom the war had been fought. He says,

> 'A woman's behaviour is what protects her modesty – not a home, nor fine clothes, nor high walls and honours such as these! Women can be seen in public in times of calamities and emergencies, in times of war, at their own weddings and at religious rituals. A war has just been fought on Sita's account. She faces a crisis in her life. There is nothing wrong if she is seen in public, especially in my presence! Bring Sita here quickly, Vibhishana! Let her see me surrounded by all my friends!' (Sattar, chap. 67)

By any account, Rama's speech at this point is surprising. He begins with a tautology about a woman's modesty, which seems out of place until one realizes that it reveals his greatest anxiety – what did Sita do, those many months away from him, captive as she was to one of the most compelling and magnificent creatures that the three worlds had ever known? How had she behaved – had she been unfaithful? Had she been tempted? Had Ravana touched her? Moreover, by speaking first about a woman's modesty, Rama is suggesting that her captivity in another man's house, and thereby her implicated virtue, makes it no longer necessary for her to be treated like a respectable woman. Because the world is no longer certain of Sita's fidelity, she can be seen in public like a common woman. He then proceeds to justify his forcing her into public at such a delicate moment, going as far as to say that this situation was a calamity, that Sita was facing a crisis in her life. But surely, with her rescue and the death of Ravana, the crisis in Sita's life is just over. Her husband stands before her and she has come through the ordeal of separation and loneliness. What crisis is Rama talking of, if not his own? The crisis he faces is quite simply this: What must he do now? Give in to the suspicion that clouds his mind, or surrender to the unbearable love he feels for her and take her back without a moment's hesitation? Or, with his kingship in mind and shadowed by the infatuation that had destroyed his father's reputation, prove that he can live without Sita, who some might suspect had given in to Ravana's pressure, if not his ample charms?

> Vibhishana wondered what Rama had in mind but he quietly did as he was told. Lakshmana, Sugriva and Hanuman were all very disturbed when they heard Rama's

> sharp words. They felt sure that he was angry with Sita because of what he had said and because he showed no desire to see his wife.
>
> Deeply embarrassed and shrinking into herself, Sita approached her husband ... When she found herself in the presence of such a huge crowd, she covered her face in shame ... She gazed at her beloved husband who was like a god to her and her face lit up with love, pleasure and wonder. Her weariness and sorrow fell away ... (Sattar, chap. 67)[9]

When Rama confronts the moment of his reunion with Sita 'joy, depression and anger flooded over him' in contrast with Sita, whose 'face lit up with love, pleasure and wonder'. Sita's dismay at the cold reception from her husband is understandable as even Rama's allies and his brother are taken aback, first that he seemed in no hurry to see her at all, and second, that for this most intimate of reunions, he would want to see her in public. Sita cannot believe what is happening to her or what she is hearing when Rama declares that he fought the war to avenge the insult to himself.

---

[9] One cannot help but think of Draupadi in the Mahabharata at the moment of her disrobing at the climax of the dice game. Sita's shame and humiliation at being brought out into public reminds us of this other more overt violation of a woman's modesty in a public space. In keeping with the more visceral tenor of the Mahabharata, Draupadi's clothes are torn off her body. While the lyrical Ramayana presents the same horror with greater gentleness, within the story and Sita's circumstance the emotional violence of the moment is no less.

> Sita's doe-like eyes filled with tears as Rama spoke. But the more he looked at her, the angrier Rama became, blazing like a fire when ghee is poured upon it. He frowned and glared at Sita, speaking to her cruelly in front of all the rakshasas and the monkeys.
>
> 'I have done my duty by rescuing you from the enemy and avenging the insult to myself. You should know that this war ... was not fought for your sake ... I have terrible suspicions about your character and conduct. The sight of you is as painful to me as a lamp to a man with diseased eyes!
>
> 'You are free to go wherever you want. The world is open to you. I have no more use for you, Sita! How can a man born into a noble family lovingly take back a woman who has lived in the house of a strange man? I am proud of my noble lineage. How can I take you back when Ravana has touched you and you have lived under his lustful gaze? ... I do not want you any more. You can go where you like ... go to Lakshmana or Bharata or to anyone else who pleases you! To Sugriva, the king of the monkeys. Or to Vibhishana, the king of the rakshasas. Go wherever you want. Ravana was aware of your beauty and your good looks. He cannot have kept you in his house for so long without touching you!' (Sattar, chap. 67)

The harshness of Rama's words is apparent to all who are present. Their terrible inappropriateness (to a wife who has suffered deeply in captivity and has remained faithful), when he tells Sita to go to another man – any other man, including her brothers-in-law – is laced with an unexpected cruelty. Nothing that we know of Rama thus far prepares us for this kind of emotional brutality and we have to look for reasons why Rama, usually so controlled in his responses to the most difficult situations, might speak and act like this.

One reason could well lie in the legacy of shame that Rama has chosen to carry from his father's last, befuddled decree. Somewhere along the way, Rama has resolved never to be accused of the same weakness – the love for a woman that clouds judgement. At this critical juncture, when he has to reclaim the woman who will be his consort as he returns in triumph to his kingdom, he cannot be seen to have given up propriety for the sake of love. In fact, when the gods gather to watch Sita step into the fire and she is restored to Rama by Agni, Rama says to them, 'Sita had to be vindicated in the eyes of the world because this lovely woman had lived inside Ravana's palace for such a long time. If I had not subjected her to such a test, good people would have said Rama, the son of Dasharatha, is blinded by his love for a woman!' (Sattar, chap. 67).

Valmiki's story of Rama is bracketed by the Bala Kanda and the Uttara Kanda, which are now commonly believed to have been composed later than the five middle books of the Ramayana.[10] The Bala Kanda tells us about an incident in Rama's

---

[10] The Bala Kanda and the Uttara Kanda are the books in which the idea of Rama's divinity is articulated and developed, as is the role that Valmiki plays in the story that he tells. As such, these two – the first and last books of the Ramayana – frame the dramatic inner narrative of love and loss, of honour and betrayal. It is here that we learn why things happened the way they did, but with great delicacy. We are

early life when Vishvamitra takes him to kill the yakshi Tataka. On this journey, they reach the arid and deserted hermitage of the sage Gautama where Rama hears the story of Ahalya, her wilful adultery and her awful punishment. He is also told that it is his presence that will restore her to her human form.[11] In the very first moments of Rama's public life, we find him faced with a situation where a woman has been unchaste, a situation that exposes the young prince to the crippling emotions of cuckolding, sexual jealousy and humiliation.

Gautama's reaction to his wife's transgression is one of disdain and moral superiority. He remains apparently unscathed by what she has done and curses her to become disembodied, living on air until she is liberated from her senseless state by Rama. Gautama says,

> 'You shall live on air, without food, and you shall sleep on ashes. You shall be invisible to all creatures as you do penance in this hermitage. You shall be purified only when Rama, the invincible son of Dasharatha, comes to this forest. Wicked woman, when you offer hospitality to

---

also alerted to the themes and motifs that tradition has chosen to hold close.

[11] Ahalya was the beautiful wife of the sage Gautama. Indra, the king of the gods, desired her and, one day, he took the form of her husband and asked her to sleep with him. Even though Ahalya recognized Indra in his disguise as her husband, she chose to make love to him. As Indra was leaving the hermitage, Gautama saw him and, through the power of his austerities, he knew what had happened. He cursed both Indra and Ahalya before going away into the mountains.

> Rama, you will be freed from your lust and passion. You shall regain your earlier form in my presence!' Gautama left the hermitage and went to a beautiful peak in the Himalayas to practise austerities. (Sattar, chap. 9)

Why is the story of Ahalya told in the Ramayana? Why is it told in this book (which was composed later) and at this stage in Rama's life? We could argue that this story, about a married woman's transgression, sets the pitch, like the drone that hums in the background for a more complex and nuanced piece of music that will emerge from a single note – that the text is anxious about women and their control over their own sexuality. Very soon after this, Rama will be faced with the consequences of another woman's sexual powers as his father succumbs to the wishes of Kaikeyi. Dasharatha is in the thrall of his young wife's charms – his sons and palace retainers (Manthara, for example) are aware of this. Kaikeyi herself also knows that she can bend the king to her slightest whim and uses her power over him to extract the boons that will make her son king. Rama's proximity to the consequences of Ahalya's infidelity and his intimacy with his father's infatuation show him two ways of dealing with women's sexual desires and powers: Gautama's example is one of rejection and retribution and, finally, honour, while Dasharatha's is one of submission, resignation and dishonour. When Rama finds himself in the position where he has to pass judgement on his wife who has lived in the house of another man, these are the choices that he has before him. Loath to be ridiculed like his father and perhaps incapable of the cold detachment of Gautama, he chooses to reject his wife twice.

It may be true that the sage Gautama never loved Ahalya and was able to walk off into the mountains without looking back, but Dasharatha and Rama both loved their wives, and the choices they make as kings in relation to these beloved wives are what add a tragic dimension to this heroic tale. Unlike his father, Rama will prove that his duty as a king comes before his personal love. Rama will ask for a test of his wife's chastity and eventually abandon her as conclusively as Gautama left Ahalya to her cursed fate.

In Valmiki's story, the trial by fire after the war exonerates Sita and the Yuddha Kanda ends with Rama's triumphal return to Ayodhya and his restoration to the throne. But the Uttara Kanda places Sita once again in the realm of doubt when town gossip about the time she spent in captivity reaches Rama's ears. She is pregnant, ready to bear Rama an heir to the throne, which is perhaps why the anxiety about her fidelity is heightened. This time, Rama treats the calumny against Sita as a criticism of himself, a criticism that he, as king, can neither afford nor abide. Rama calls for all his brothers and sadly tells them of the decision that he has made.

> 'Commoners as well as prominent citizens hold me in contempt. I find that very painful. I was born into the great and noble family of the Ikshvakus ... In the presence of the gods and the gandharvas in Lanka, she was given back to me after she had been declared pure. I knew in my heart that the virtuous woman was innocent and so I accepted her and brought her back to Ayodhya.
>
> 'But now, the terrible things that people are saying make me unhappy. An infamous man who is the subject

> of common discourse goes to the hells of the unrighteous and stays there as long as the story of his disgrace is told. The gods do not love the notorious and even the world loves a man who is well spoken of. Good men's deeds are motivated by a desire for fame. I would give up my life, even renounce all of you, for fear of a scandal. How can I hesitate or do anything less in Sita's case?' (Sattar, chap. 69)

With that, Rama commands Lakshmana to take Sita into the forest and leave her there to fend for herself as best she can.

On both occasions when Rama has to reject Sita (in Lanka and then in Ayodhya), he mentions his family and its nobility. After the war, he says, 'How can a man born into a noble family lovingly take back a woman who has lived in the house of a strange man? I am proud of my noble lineage.' And in Ayodhya, Rama reminds his brothers that he was 'born into the great and noble family of the Ikshvakus'. Further, when the gods return Sita to him in Lanka, he says that he had allowed the public test of chastity because otherwise people would have said that 'Rama, son of Dasharatha, was blinded by his love for a woman.' Rama is clearly worried about what people will think and say about his beloved wife and, by extension about him, whatever he might feel about her innocence. And because he chooses to mention his lineage (which must include his father) both times, we can be persuaded that Rama carries the burden of his father's folly and that he is determined to compensate for it at any cost. This decision is personal as well as political: he, Rama, will not be tarred with the same brush as his father in terms of his personal reputation, and he will bow to the wishes of his subjects.

The third separation from Sita, however, brings Rama back into the realm of his private life and loss. Rama's sons, Lava and Kusha, are sent by Valmiki to recite the story of Rama at their father's great sacrifice. The boys sing the marvellous tale to public acclaim and are eventually taken before their father. When Rama realizes that he is listening to his own story and from his sons, he asks that Sita be brought back from the forest where he had sent her. She returns and the sage Valmiki vouches for her virtue, accusing Rama of being afraid of a little gossip. Again, Rama says that he has never doubted Sita and that:

> 'Sita has already declared her innocence before the gods. And I abandoned her, even though I knew she was innocent, because I feared a scandal. You must forgive me for that. And I know that these twin boys are my sons. When Sita proves her innocence before the world, I shall be able to love her again!' (Sattar, chap. 70)

The years of separation from Sita must have taken their toll as Rama seems to have forgotten how to love her. First besieged by fears for her safety and concerned about her continuing love for him when she was abducted by Ravana, then beset by longing and the pressures of righteous kingship when he sends her away into the forest, Rama has sacrificed his inner emotions for his public kingship. But let us consider more carefully how Rama reacts when he prepares to meet Sita after his victory over Ravana. At first, he is silent and his eyes fill with tears. He experiences 'joy, depression and anger'. The 'joy' is at seeing her again, relatively safe and unharmed, her love for him apparent and her constancy equally so. But why does Rama feel depressed and angry? Where are the tears coming from? I would argue that he is sad because he knows that he has to humiliate her, his sweet, innocent beloved, in public by asking for proof of her chastity, that his imminent life as a king demands this and nothing less. Rama loves Sita more than anyone else in the world – his demented grief when he returns from chasing the magic deer in the forest and finds her gone is proof of that, as is his anguish in the rainy season as he waits for the skies to clear and the search for Sita to begin. His anger is at the public life that has claimed him, a life where he believes that it is necessary to prove that he is not like his father, that for him, dharma comes before love. From this moment onwards, Rama will be forever the king, placing public duty before his personal feelings. How his heart must have shattered into a thousand pieces as he spoke those cruel worlds to gentle Sita on the battlefield!

But when the second occasion of doubt over Sita's fidelity arises, Rama does not express grief or anger. In the intervening months between the victory in Lanka and his ascension to the throne of Ayodhya, his kingship has claimed him fully. The people of Ayodhya and the reputation of the Ikshvaku dynasty are of primary importance. This time, there is not even a trial for Sita to prove her innocence – Rama makes a swift and unilateral decision to banish her into the forest where she had been so happy, telling his brothers that they are not to question him or argue with him. He is even willing to put aside the fact that he has never doubted Sita (a fact he mentions over and over again) just so that he can prove to the world that he is not besotted, that he is still capable of thinking unemotionally about his wife.

The people of Ayodhya will not have occasion to say again that their king loves his wife more than he loves dharma.

Does Rama's heart break again on this second occasion? He does not ask for proof, he does not even tell Sita himself that he has banished her. Lakshmana is assigned the task of taking her to the forest and leaving her there, that too, under false pretences, for Sita is told that she is going to visit the wives of the sages who had become her friends during their time in the forest. Perhaps Rama cannot put himself through another moment of confrontation with her, nor can he bear to humiliate her again in public, in front of her own people. Perhaps he knows that he will weaken if he were to tell her himself, for he loves her still. Perhaps he would not be able to bear her unspoken criticism as he bows to the will of the people at a time when he should defend her with the truth that has been proven in Lanka and which is the same truth that he holds in his heart – that despite murderous threats and lavish promises from Ravana, she never stopped loving Rama and that she remained faithful to him in every sense of the word.

Or, like others, does Rama doubt Sita, especially now that she is pregnant? Is it this doubt that makes it possible for him to let her go, potentially forever? His remarks when she returns with Valmiki are telling. He says that once Sita has proved her innocence before the world (despite the fact that he has always believed in her and he knows that Lava and Kusha are his sons), he will be able to 'love her again'. Where has Rama's love gone, in all those barren years of being the righteous (but lonely) king? Did he harden his heart so much to abandon Sita that he cannot now remember what it is to love her? Or did he cease to love her in the years that she was away in Valmiki's ashrama, as he built a life around her absence? I believe that Rama had hardened his heart for their second separation, knowing that Sita's absence would devastate him. Surely the most difficult moment of his life was to send her away again because of a promise he had made to himself about his public conduct. He had spent years suppressing his love for her and when she returns with Valmiki and he has the chance to be with her again, he must rediscover the parts of himself that he had buried under his heavy crown. Rama's tragedy is that he never gets the opportunity to do that, for this time it is Sita who decides that she cannot be with him any longer. She enters the earth, never to return, leaving Rama desolate and alone, his worst fears of a life without her having come true.

Why does the Uttara Kanda destroy the happy ending of the Yuddha Kanda with the addition of Sita's banishment? For all intents and purposes, the story of Rama could well have ended with the triumphal return to Ayodhya, his coronation, a happily-ever-after with his brothers and Sita who is sure to bear him heirs. The Uttara Kanda is full of 'corrective' stories, or stories that fill in the gaps, answer the questions that linger from the stories that we already know from the previous books of the Ramayana. Why did Ravana, powerful and headstrong as he was, not take Sita against her will? Because, the Uttara Kanda tells us, when he had forced himself upon the apsara Rambha, she had cursed him that his heads would explode if he were to do the same to any other woman. Why did Hanuman not know of his great powers and immense abilities until Jambavan reminded him of them before his momentous leap across the ocean? The Uttara Kanda tell us it is because when Hanuman was still a young monkey, newly empowered by all his boons from the gods, he harassed sages who were conducting sacrifices. They cursed him to forget all his special powers until he was reminded of them at a time when they would be most useful.

So, why is it that Sita's story needs to be reopened in the Uttara Kanda? What are the unanswered questions and the doubts that linger from all that has happened before? Is it because we need to be reassured that Lava and Kusha are, indeed, Rama's sons, established as such in public by Valmiki who has divine vision? Or is the text still dealing with the anxiety about women and their sexual desire that was suggested by the Ahalya story in the Bala Kanda?[12] Unlike Ahalya who chose to surrender to the charms of another man, Sita was abducted and, against all odds, she remained both faithful and unharmed. The consequence of Ahalya's choice, of her acting on her desire for another man, is the curse that destroys her body, the seat of her pleasure. In Sita's case, there has been no choice – as she herself says in that horrendous moment at the end of the war, when Rama publicly insults her: 'If my body was touched by another man, it was not because I wanted it! Destiny must bear the responsibility for that. My heart, the only thing I could control, was always with you. What could I do about the other

[12] The similarities between Ahalya and Sita have been noticed by many, and the works of a number of contemporary women writers create situations where the two women meet and talk about how they have been treated by their spouses and by the male-dominated worlds in which they live.

parts of my body that were subject to the will of others?' (Sattar, chap. 67). Why, then, are there these suspicions about her? Is it because Ravana was irresistible or because he was capable of taking her against her will? We already have the story about Ravana being restrained by Rambha's curse, which explains why he did not assault Sita. It would seem, then, that the lingering doubts that the text feels about the story are precisely about Sita's potential to choose and to act on her desire, as Ahalya had done. And it is to banish this doubt once and for all that Sita must endure this terrible second separation, one that climaxes in her final departure from Rama's life.

The Bala Kanda and the Uttara Kanda frame the story of Rama and his righteousness within more complex issues about the righteousness of women. Women's righteousness, not surprisingly, is constructed around their sexual behaviour within and without marriage. While Ahalya is fundamentally transgressive in seeking and choosing her own pleasure and is brutally punished, Sita is wrongfully accused and punished in an equally cruel manner as her banishment suggests to all that she has, in fact, transgressed. But while Ahalya returns to the fold, as it were, once her curse ends, it is Sita who breaks through her conjugal bonds and abandons her husband forever.

We have been taught to admire Rama for being a paragon of virtue, for being the perfect man, equanimous in the face of all adversity, true to his inner convictions, no matter how much they seem to be at odds with the feelings of those around him. When he speaks, Rama constantly takes refuge in the idea of dharma to explain his choices to others, as if he were always sure of what is right. But if we see Rama as less than equanimous, if we see him as a man who has to rise above the torment in his heart in order to do what is right, rather than as a man to whom doing the right thing comes easily and naturally, surely that makes him even more admirable. It could be that because Dasharatha's final act as king is seen by all as adharma, Rama is forced to resort to the rhetoric of dharma to restore a sense of order. It may well be that he was never convinced of the rightness of what he did in terms of his own life and happiness – witness his anguish when he has to reject Sita in Lanka in front of his friends and allies, his inability to tell her about her banishment and his plaintive hope that he will have the chance to love her again with all his heart once she has finally been proven innocent in Ayodhya. What Rama has to live with for the rest of his life is the knowledge that his actions forced the woman he loved (and who had loved him with such tenderness and devotion) to leave him. In seeking the confirmation of his own righteousness through his wife's reputation and predicating that righteousness on the sacrifice of his personal happiness, he has lost what mattered most to him. Not only has he lost his beloved, he has foregone the capacity to surrender to love.

THE MATTED LOCKS OF THE ASCETIC AND THE WEAPONS OF THE WARRIOR

Rama's reaction to his father's decree that he shall be banished into the forest has many stages and moments. As he gets over the initial shock, which he manfully conceals from those he loves and who love him, he begins to formulate an attitude that will carry him through the fourteen long years he must spend away from the kingdom and away from what had, until then, seemed to be a secure and certain destiny as king.

Rama's immediate reaction when he hears about the boons that Kaikeyi has claimed for herself is:

> 'I say again to reassure you that I will gladly live the life of an ascetic in the forest. How can I refuse to do this when it is my father who asks? ... You must convince my father that I will do this without sadness ... You know that I am like a rishi in my devotion to dharma. I would do anything to please my father. There is no greater dharma than service to one's father and obedience to his wishes.' (Sattar, chap. 15)

When Rama repeats the news to his mother, Lakshmana and Sita, he continues to declare that he is happy to go to the forest and that at this point, what is important is dharma, which he defines as obedience to his father's wishes. Rama is choosing his dharma as a son over all the other choices available to him at that moment. Kaushalya and Lakshmana try to persuade him that it is equally his dharma to undo an unrighteous act, to overthrow the king so that Kaikeyi's outrageous demands come to naught. But Rama remains steadfast in his own understanding of his duty, which is to go to the forest for fourteen years and then return to claim the kingdom.

Rama is perhaps aware that, while his personal dharma as a son, a husband and a brother is clear, the foundations of his dharma as a public person are no longer as stable and obvious as they were. In this confusion, he repeatedly says that the pursuit of dharma is the highest pursuit of all, much higher and more valuable than the pursuit of wealth and pleasure. It is the pursuit of the latter two that forms the basis of his criticism of Dasharatha, but it would appear that Rama renounces wealth and pleasure also for the sake of exploring, in as uncluttered a way as possible, what dharma might be. The forest provides him with this time, away from public duties and the demands of kingship.

When Rama is ready to depart for the forest with Lakshmana and Sita, they go to seek Dasharatha's blessings. The old king begs Rama to arrest him and overturn the command that would banish him, but Rama speaks with confidence about his decision to leave.

> 'I desire neither the kingdom nor happiness, not even Sita. I wish only that your honour be maintained ... I am not interested in worldly pleasures or in desire, or even in

> those that are dear to me. Do not grieve on my account ... I shall be happy in the forest, living on roots and fruits.' (Sattar, chap. 18)

In the short time between hearing of his banishment and his farewell to his father, and amidst the fraught emotions of his leave-taking from his mother, Rama has managed to formulate a statement of what would serve him best during his exile: he has renounced the kingdom and his ties to his loved ones, symbolizing his renunciation of wealth and pleasure. A more fitting preparation for life as an ascetic would be hard to find. Rama understands the hardships that lie ahead of him and identifies the very attachments that will make those trials harder to bear. Having taken the support of dharma to help him obey his father, he now wants to put himself in a mental state that will allow him to endure the consequences of that decision.

Trying desperately to make sense of the huge breach in his life, Rama also considers fate as an explanation for what has happened to him. He does not seek a karmic explanation for his trials, though he does understand that it is boons and curses that have bound Dasharatha to this terrible deed. Even before this bold statement in public of renouncing the kingdom, wealth and pleasure, Rama has a heated discussion with Lakshmana about why he will not fight the king's decree. Lakshmana refuses to believe that Rama would respect the word of their father who has clearly made the wrong decision. Since the argument of following dharma and obeying Dasharatha does not make any impression on Lakshmana and Kaushalya, Rama goes beyond personal decisions and choices and resorts to an argument from a grander design.

> 'Lakshmana, you have to see destiny at work in my exile and in the reversal of the kingship that was entrusted to me. How could Kaikeyi have worked against me unless it was destiny that directed her to do so? ... That which is unthinkable and which cannot be countered by any creature is an act of destiny ... Where is the man who can fight against fate which is manifest only in its workings? Joy and sorrow, fear and anger, gain and loss, existence and non-existence – destiny reveals itself in all these things.' (Sattar, chap. 16)

Lakshmana's response is fierce and aggressive.

> 'How can a man like you, who stands so strong and proud in the dharma of a kshatriya, sing praises of this thing called destiny. Fate is the refuge of the weak and the impotent ... I feel only contempt for a dharma that makes even someone as resolute as you vacillate like this! It is your attachment to dharma that confuses you.
>
> 'I cannot accept that all this happened because of fate. An explanation like that is for cowards, not for the brave! No capable man would ever be oppressed by the workings of destiny. And a real man would never allow fate to frustrate his aims. I will show you which is stronger, fate or manliness. The people will see that fate, which reversed your consecration, has been defeated by my courage.' (Sattar, chap. 16)

Lakshmana makes a complex argument, suggesting that the dharma of a kshatriya would not allow a man to bow to fate while the personal dharma that Rama seems to have adopted for this moment weakens him and enables him to surrender to the dictates of destiny. It is almost as if, in Lakshmana's world, kshatriya dharma demands that you take on fate and make your own destiny. Moments earlier, Rama had admonished Lakshmana: 'Give up your ignoble ideas inspired by the duties of a kshatriya! Follow my example. Take refuge in dharma and not in violence!' (Sattar, chap. 16). Both brothers are citing dharma for the course of action that they prefer and it would seem that both are quite clear about which dharma – the public/caste dharma as against the private/personal dharma – they are using as a justification for the course of action they prefer.

Perhaps it is this altercation that makes Rama realize that he has to consider the implications of kshatriya dharma for the rest of his life, and not just for the period of the exile. Rama's life in the forest with Sita and Lakshmana becomes the existential space within which he re-examines his dharma and tries to understand the pulls and pushes of his public destiny and his private aspirations. He tries to place these duties and obligations within a realm of action that is bound by fate, and it would appear that he is willing to take on the hand that fate has dealt him, albeit in surprising ways. Once Sita is abducted and his life is propelled once again into action, Rama cannot fully embody what he has taught himself during the quiet periods between his battles with rakshasas in Dandaka.

The way Rama has lived as a king in waiting in the palaces of Ayodhya cannot be the way he will live in the forest. Kaikeyi's terms of banishment contain the clause that he must live as an ascetic in the forest, that he must renounce his princely habits and live a life of simplicity and abstinence. In fact, when Rama, Lakshmana and Sita come to say goodbye to the old king, she is the one who eagerly thrusts their ascetic robes at them. One may presume here that when Rama does take on the additional challenge of living like an ascetic in the forest, he has to put aside his kshatriya dharma until he returns to Ayodhya.

Rama enters into the rigours of asceticism consciously and in stages. The first moment of initiation is when Kaikeyi hands them all robes of bark as they say farewell to Dasharatha. On their first night away from the city, while they are still with Sumantra, the royal charioteer, Rama says that he will drink only water and fast through the night. The next evening, they meet Guha, the chieftain of the region that borders the forest, and he offers them food and drink. Rama says,

> 'I thank you for all the gifts you have brought with so much affection, but I cannot accept them. You know that I have taken the vows of an ascetic. I must live in the forest, wear simple clothes and eat only fruits and roots according to the ascetics' code of conduct. I can accept nothing other than fodder for the horses.' (Sattar, chap. 20)

Later, as the brothers and Sita prepare to go further into the forest, Rama says to Guha,

> 'I must mat my hair. Bring me the sap of the nyagrodha tree.' Guha fetched the sap and Rama matted his own hair as well as Lakshmana's with it. But even with their matted

> hair and their simple clothes, the brothers shone like rishis. Rama took the required vows, and thus it was that Rama and Lakshmana took their first steps along the ascetics' path. (Sattar, chap. 20)

Already we have a sense of disjunction between the way the brothers appear and who they really are, even when they are suitably attired for their new lives. Further, when Guha recounts this same moment to Bharata a few days later as Bharata arrives in search of Rama, he says,

> 'I brought Rama many different kinds of food as refreshment. He was gracious, but in keeping with the kshatriya code, he refused to accept any gifts from me. "It is our duty to give and not to accept gifts" is what he said to us with great courtesy as he turned down our offerings. He drank only the water that Lakshmana brought him, and then he and Sita fasted for the night.' (Sattar, chap. 24)

This lapse in the behaviour of an ascetic on Rama's part can be accounted for by the newness of his role and the habits of his princely past, where to receive gifts was anathema.

From the moment he dons his ascetic's robes to the moment when he unequivocally rejects kshatriya dharma, Rama has passed through various stages, as we have seen. Each stage of his preparatory mental process has been marked by one more addition to his ascetics' code – the fasting, the matted hair, the taking of the vows – as if he were building himself up to this enormous challenge of changing his life and his instincts, both externally and internally. But for each ascetic virtue that Rama takes on, he seems unable to shed an equivalent kshatriya quality. He is still carrying his magnificent weapons, is still eating meat and he is still in the company of his beloved wife.

These are some of the fundamentally mixed signals that the brothers send out to those whom they meet in the forest, in their early days as well as over the years: they are accompanied by a woman and they are fully armed. The weapons that Rama and Lakshmana carry into the forest are carefully selected and cared for. When they are preparing to leave the palace, Rama tells Lakshmana which weapons from their extensive personal armouries they need to take with them. 'The two divine bows that strike terror into the hearts of all that see them ... as well as the two impenetrable coats of mail, the inexhaustible quivers of arrows and the two gold-hilted swords that shine like the sun – fetch them all from our teacher's house' (Sattar, chap. 18). The weapons are used to kill animals for food, another violation of the newly adopted ascetics' code, but they are also to protect the princes and Sita from the dangers of the forest.

When Bharata comes to the forest to plead with Rama to take his rightful place on the throne, he approaches the hut where his brothers and Sita have made their home.

> Inside the hut, Bharata could see his brothers' mighty bows and arrows, equal to the weapons of Indra himself. They were adorned with gold and blazed with such splendour that they would make their enemies tremble. Even the arrows with their gleaming tips in their quivers shone like rays of the sun. Swords glistened in their golden scabbards

> and shields were decorated with gold designs ... Bharata had to look hard before he saw Rama sitting in a corner, his matted locks piled on top of his head. The lord of the earth, who had always walked the path of the righteous, was seated on the skin of a black antelope. (Sattar, chap. 25)

Like others who do not know the princes, Bharata's first impression is that these are warriors, fully armed and resplendent in their martial glory. Other descriptions (like the one above) mention that even with their matted hair, which is the definitive sign of an ascetic, they look like rishis. Whoever they may be, they are not ordinary forest-dwelling ascetics. There are two other incidents when these contrary signs are noticed by those who meet the princes. When Shurpanakha comes upon them in Dandaka, her first words to Rama are: 'Your hair is matted like an ascetic's but you carry a bow and arrow and you are in the company of a woman!' (Sattar, chap. 29). After Sita has been abducted and Rama and Lakshmana enter Kishkindha in search of her, Hanuman approaches them with a similar question on his lips.

> 'You enhance the brilliance of these shining waters with your shining skin! But who are you, dressed like this in the clothes of ascetics? You seem to have the valour of lions. You are armed with bows that rival Indra's, you are as handsome and powerful as bulls, your arms are as mighty as elephants' trunks ... but what are you doing here? You are clearly warriors, but your eyes are like lotus petals and you have the matted locks of ascetics!' (Sattar, chap. 35)

It is precisely these simultaneous signs of contradiction – the warrior and the ascetic – that circumscribe Rama's time in the forest and give us an indication of the inner conflict that he must resolve. Who is he going to be, in the forest and after? He has already decided in some way, perhaps out of despair at ever understanding how life moves, that fate has led him into this situation where the public dharma that he grew up with and took for granted is no longer certain and is certainly not appropriate for the circumstances in which he finds himself. As he says to a reluctant Bharata in his discourse on kingship, 'No man can do exactly as he pleases, for he is not his own master. His fate drags him hither and thither' (Sattar, chap. 26). Rama uses this opportunity he has been afforded by an apparently capricious fate to think about what it means to be a kshatriya, a warrior defined by violence, righteous or otherwise. He has already suggested to Lakshmana that his anger comes out of his position as a kshatriya and that he should renounce both his position and his anger and follow dharma (obviously, a dharma other than the one that Lakshmana is standing by) and non-violence.

In a remarkable speech to the sage Vasishtha, who has accompanied Bharata to the forest to persuade Rama to return to Ayodhya, Rama says,

> 'It is clear to me that every man must hold to the truth, that is his dharma. It is for this reason alone that ascetics command so much respect. I renounce the dharma of a kshatriya because it is fundamentally unrighteous even though it has some good things about it. It attracts the

> cruel, the base, the greedy and those inclined to be wicked.' (Sattar, chap. 26)

In the relatively short time between his exhortation to Lakshmana, a few hours before their departure from the city, and Bharata's arrival in Nandigram, Rama has rejected kshatriya dharma as unrighteous twice, first privately to Lakshmana, and now in the presence of Ayodhya's royal court.

Rama seems to have become aware that it was the conflict between his father's public role as a king and his private role as a husband, and the resulting choice, that led to the calamity that befell his most favoured son. The public role as a king is, no doubt, dictated by kshatriya dharma, and the boons that Dasharatha had to uphold were on his honour as a husband. If Dasharatha had not been a king, his choice would not have had such devastating consequences and so, it is in the light of Dasharatha's kingship that we see how inappropriate the choice was. Perhaps that is where Rama's rejection of kshatriya dharma as potentially unrighteous comes from – the understanding that even a good king could be a bad father, brother or husband. More than that, that whichever dharma one chooses as the wellspring of action, someone will be harmed. For the knowing reader, the fact that Rama is going to be called upon to make similar choices between his public and private selves at the end of his exile only heightens the poignancy of Rama's realization.

In the early days in the forest, Rama is impressed with the simple humility of the lives of the sages, and Sita is equally moved by the gentleness and generosity of the sages' wives who treat her like a daughter. Moreover, Rama sees the tranquillity that defines the lives of the sages as well as their relationships with their wives who are companions, rather than sexual partners. This gives him a new way to perceive his relationship with Sita, a way that is different from the passionate relationships of the Ayodhya court which had changed the course of his life. The sages' lives show Rama that love and detachment can be simultaneously present and when he endures his most trying times in terms of his love for Sita, it is this paradigm that he looks to for strength and inspiration.

Although in the Aranya Kanda, Sita is more a wife and more dependent on her husband and brother-in-law than at any other time in the story, it is here that we see her making her most important speech to Rama when she exhorts him to give up his weapons. For perhaps the only time in the entire story we hear Sita speaking as a human being and not as a wife, a daughter or a mother. What she says to Rama reveals the ambivalence within which he is trying to live and also exposes his (as yet) unsuccessful attempt to give up the dharma into which he has been born.

Rama, Lakshmana and Sita have just left the idyllic regions where the sages live, for their presence has led to increased harassment by the rakshasas. Despite the dangers, they head deeper into the wilderness, into the Dandaka forest, sparsely inhabited by humans. Almost as soon as they enter, they are attacked by Viradha, as if in warning for all that lies ahead. Sita watches as her husband and his brother use their remarkable fighting skills to vanquish the rakshasa. After a short visit with the last of the sages, they continue onwards and Sita begins to talk. She speaks of the weaknesses that might afflict men and says,

> 'But the third weakness which men succumb to because of their passions, the inflicting of violence and cruelty upon other beings without reason or enmity, that weakness appears to be present in you now. You have promised to kill the rakshasas in combat in order to protect the sages of the Dandaka forest. This has brought you and your brother to this forest, armed with your bows and arrows.
>
> 'It disturbs me a great deal when I see you like this ... Listen and I will tell you why.
>
> 'Now that you are here with your brother and both of you are armed, you shall see many forest creatures. Inevitably, you will be tempted to use your arrows. Like dry fuel bursts into flame when it is near a fire, so too, a kshatriya's passions are ignited when he has a bow at hand ... A kshatriya should use his bow in the forest only to protect the oppressed. What a difference there is between the life of weapons and that of the forest, between the vows of a kshatriya and those of an ascetic! We must learn to respect the code of behaviour of the world we now inhabit. Here, the mind is perverted by extreme proximity to weapons. You can return to the code of the kshatriyas when we go back to Ayodhya!' (Sattar, chap. 28)

Despite Sita voicing many of the thoughts that seem to be in Rama's mind, he feels the need to defend himself and the powerful weapons that he carries.

> 'But I must remind you of what you yourself said, that kshatriyas are armed so that the cries of the oppressed may never be heard. Those resolute sages who live in the forest are being tormented ... they can no longer live in peace because of the rakshasas' wicked deeds ... I promised the sages of the Dandaka forest that I would protect them.' (Sattar, chap. 28)

The conversations about giving up the kshatriya code occur well before Rama is called upon to make a choice about whether to become a non-violent ascetic or remain the warrior prince that he has always been. Thus far, the only creature that he has killed in the forest is Viradha (Lakshmana is the one that hunts the animals for their food). The killing of Viradha is mitigated not simply by the fact that the rakshasa grabbed Sita, but also by the fact that Viradha was, in fact, a cursed gandharva who would be liberated by his death at the hands of Rama. The real tests for Rama's change of heart are in the future, in the encounter with Shurpanakha, Kabandha and, finally, with Vali. Further, once Sita is abducted and Rama hears that she has been taken by the rakshasa Ravana, he realizes that he can no longer abjure the warrior code that he was born into and for which he was trained. He knows he will have to fight a battle to win Sita back, that he will need to make military alliances and uphold the terms of those alliances, no matter what. The violence that he had so hopefully renounced in his early days in the forest will now be his constant companion as he moves inexorably towards the confrontation with his wife's abductor.

Sita's critique of the kshatriya propensity for violence echoes Rama's stated reasons for rejecting the code of the warrior. However, the two occasions when he had spoken out against his inherited dharma were both in places of safety, once in the palace and once in Nandigram. In the forest itself, Rama realizes that his renunciation of kshatriya violence was in haste and that he may need to be a kshatriya for much longer than he thought. Also, that a statement of renunciation and actually transcending the habits and instincts of the past are not the same thing. While the renunciation of violence and royal duties that go with being a prince was easy to do when the forest exile was an idea, the reality of the forest with its inherent dangers make Rama's weapons and his abilities as a warrior his most important attributes. But even as he feels the need to call upon his kshatriya training and nature, Rama has experienced the ascetic life which draws him, compelling him to contrast its simplicity with the complexities of his conflicting aspirations and contradictory emotions.

What Rama sees in the lives of the ascetics and also in his own life in the forest is the possibility of a disdain for wealth and pleasure, the eager pursuit of which has been haunting him from the moment he heard of his banishment. By giving up the kingdom (albeit temporarily), Rama has given up the pursuit of wealth and comfort, power and glory. The pursuit of pleasure and desire, however, has not been as easy to leave behind because Sita and Lakshmana are with him in the forest. As he aspires towards ascetic values, Rama understands that he has to be detached from those around him if he is to relinquish desire and the pitfalls that come with it. Since Sita and Lakshmana are the ones who are closest to him and those whom he loves the most, one assumes that this is where his greatest test for detachment lies.

Additionally, Rama and Sita's time in the forest together is particularly precious as they get to enjoy simple pleasures, away from the pomp and circumstance of the royal court. Their rustic living quarters, the birds, trees, rivers and gentle forest animals create a world of quiet love and growing emotional intimacy between the couple. And it is in these idyllic surroundings that Rama knows he has to disengage with Sita if he is to keep the promise he has made to himself – that he will renounce pleasure. There is another element in Rama's need to distance himself from Sita, and that is the shame that he carries from his father's last days. He will do anything to ensure that he is never accused of the same weakness as Dasharatha, that is, that his love for a woman blinded him to a greater duty.

Rama has already said that he would be willing to give up Sita and Lakshmana as well as the kingdom and even his own life to maintain his father's honour. But as time passes, and Sita is actually taken away from him, we hear him say that he can and will give up Sita should the occasion demand it. This despite the fact that when Viradha grabs hold of Sita, Rama astonishingly bursts into tears.

> 'Look, Lakshmana,' said Rama, his face pale as he saw his wife under the rakshasa's arm. 'This beautiful princess, the delicate daughter of Janaka, my wife ... is being forced to sit on Viradha's hip ... I cannot bear the thought of Sita

> being touched by another man! It upsets me more than the death of my father and the loss of my kingdom!' (Sattar, chap. 28)

Having realized the depth of his attachment to Sita, Rama begins the painful process of pulling away from her, of containing the great love that he feels for this fragile young woman who has followed him into the forest. That he has not succeeded in doing so for all the time that she is with him in the forest is painfully clear when we witness his mind-numbing grief at her abduction.

When Maricha has been killed and the brothers realize that something is terribly wrong, they rush to the hut where Sita had been left alone.

> 'If I go back to our settlement and find that Sita is not there to greet me with her sweet smile and her gentle words, I shall kill myself!' continued Rama ... Rama called out to Sita again and again. 'She has been abducted! She is dead! She has been eaten!' ... But though he searched high and low, Rama could not find his beloved in the forest. His eyes red from weeping, he seemed like a madman as he ran from tree to tree, from the mountains to the river, weeping more and more as he plunged deeper and deeper into an ocean of grief. (Sattar, chap. 34)

Once Sita has been taken from him, it would appear that Rama's resolve to be emotionally removed from her is strengthened and the task is made easier by her absence. Although he continues to profess his love for her during all the months of waiting in

Kishkindha and he suffers the agonies of uncertainty as he waits for the rains to end for the journey south to begin, his thoughts about her are now linked with the loss of his kingdom. As the brothers wait for Sugriva to call up his troops, Rama is overcome with sorrow again.

> He thought constantly about his abducted wife who was dearer to him than life. He would lie down every night, but the beauty of his surroundings made it impossible for him to sleep. Never really free from sadness, Rama would find his eyes brimming with tears at times like this. (Sattar, chap. 39)

By the end of the season, although Rama's grief over Sita remains unabated, his lament to Lakshmana is: 'The four months of the rainy season have gone by but for me, tormented by grief, they have seemed like a hundred years! I live here, deprived of my wife and my kingdom' (Sattar, chap. 39).

During the war, in the thick of battle, Lakshmana is felled by Indrajit's powerful arrows and appears lifeless. Rama is distraught and says,

> 'What use to me is Sita or my life when I see my brother lifeless like this on the battlefield? If I looked hard enough, I would find another woman like Sita in this world. But I would never find anyone like my brother Lakshmana, my companion and adviser!' (Sattar, chap. 59)

Later, in the penultimate battle with Ravana, Lakshmana is fatally wounded. Once again, Rama's fortitude deserts him and he says, 'What use is life and happiness to me if my beloved brother dies? ... I have no interest in fighting, or in my life, or even in Sita when my brother lies dead in battle!' (Sattar, chap. 65).

It is as if the long separation from Sita, the months of waiting, the rigours of the army's march south and the fatigue of the prolonged battle have sapped Rama's energies. Along with that, these trials seem to have made Sita and his love for her unreal. The warrior has lost his gentle nature and the tenderness that Sita brought out in him. The kshatriya in Rama has triumphed in time for him to return to his kingdom, bathed in the glory of victory, and the ascetic has been left behind in the wilderness. Hanuman is the last one to comment on the appearance of the ascetic in Rama's demeanour at their very first meeting, which was shortly after Sita's abduction. As Rama moves further away from his forest life in space and in time, his anger returns as well. However justified the reappearance of these qualities and emotions may be, they are exactly what Rama was seeking to lose when he came to the forest.

If, indeed, Rama is seeking a life of quietude and contemplation, the demands made on him as a warrior must surely be irksome. Beyond that, he has begun to understand that whatever direction he chooses for himself, it is a warrior and a prince that he will always be to the world. As he seeks a dharma that will allow him to fulfil all his duties equitably, he is being pushed further and further into the public realm where his actions impact the lives of more and more creatures. His stated desire to renounce the powers and obligations of kingship has come to naught, even in his exile away from the kingdom.

It is this uncomfortable space between his inner aspirations and the public destiny which shadows him that Rama has to negotiate during his exile. Deeply attracted to the values of detachment, he believes that they will make him a better man, better able to uphold the personal dharma that he seeks for himself, a dharma that will allow him to discharge public and private obligations with equal felicity. But he finds that it will never be so – the intervention of fate that he saw as giving him a chance to negotiate his place in the world has turned out to be nothing other than the destiny that binds him to an inevitable and irrevocable public role as a warrior and then as a king.

A TALE OF THREE CITIES AND THE SEARCH FOR DHARMA

There are effectively three worlds in Valmiki's Ramayana, each located in and defined by a city: Ayodhya, Kishkindha and Lanka. Each of the cities reflects the nature of the beings that inhabit it, each of them embodies the characteristics of its peoples. By depicting each of the cities as having a unique milieu, the Ramayana also explores multiple dharmas, or ways of being in the world. Kishkindha and Lanka are set in contrast to Ayodhya just as monkey and rakshasa dharmas are contrasted with the human codes of behaviour and ethics lived out by Rama and his brothers. There is, of course, a fourth world in the story, the liminal world of the forest, where ways of being collide and the way one lives and follows dharma appears to be a matter of choice. It is here that Rama is able to think about renouncing the (human) kshatriya dharma that he was born into and adopting another dharma. In the cities, however, ways of being and doing are determined and unalterable.

In the opening chapters of the Bala Kanda, where Narada tells Valmiki the story of Rama, he describes Rama and the city of Ayodhya thus:

> 'The townspeople were glad to have him back. Rama's presence made them virtuous, free of sickness, famine,

> fear and danger. No one had to witness the death of their sons, no woman was widowed and they all lived lives of devotion to their husbands. There was no fear of storms, nor of death by water, nor fear of fire nor plague nor fever ... Rama performed all the necessary rituals and sacrifices, including the ashvamedha sacrifice ... The prestige of his royal clan increased a hundredfold because of his deeds and all the four castes remained dedicated to their duties in this world.' (Sattar, chap. 1)

The descriptions of Ayodhya are relatively minimal, the city being defined more by references to the nature of its people and the order that prevails in it rather than by its buildings. The most important thing about Ayodhya is the maintenance of order (which includes the four castes behaving as they should) that is consequent upon the righteousness of its rulers and the upholding of dharma. What we see of the city itself is by the way.

Dasharatha rules the kingdom of Kosala from his capital city, Ayodhya. He is a wise and just king, an upholder of dharma. In the Ayodhya Kanda, he announces that his eldest son, Rama, will succeed him as king in Ayodhya for he has grown old and worn. When the citizens of Ayodhya hear about Rama's coronation, they are delighted and

> the joyous citizens began to decorate the city. Banners and buntings danced in the breeze from temple spires that gleamed like white clouds, from the homes and terraces of

> rich and prominent citizens, from roads and city squares, from private homes and public buildings. Even the tallest trees were decorated with brightly coloured flags ... Flowers were scattered in the streets, sweet incense filled the air and wooden torches as large as trees lined the main roads. (Sattar, chap. 13)

At other moments, as we follow Rama from palace to palace as he hears about and then conveys the news of his banishment, we see the city as a backdrop and we learn that Dasharatha's palace 'shone like the peaks of Mount Kailasha'. And Rama looked upon 'his prosperous city, its squares and highways crowded with horses and elephants and chariots and its people who displayed their abundant wealth, lined with shops overflowing with goods for sale, and he felt proud and happy' (Sattar, chap. 15).

While there is wealth and prosperity in Ayodhya, there is an atmosphere of restraint and virtue, of whiteness and purity, of gleaming spires and orderly squares and streets. The only moment of chaos we experience in Ayodhya is when Rama, Sita and Lakshmana depart for the forest.

> As Rama drove out of Ayodhya for his long stay in the forest, the city was filled with the sounds of horses' trappings jingling, of elephants trumpeting, of agitated people. The sounds swelled and reverberated as the entire city, old and young, ran behind Rama's chariot as they would run towards water in the parched months of the summer. (Sattar, chap. 19)

As an example of the character of the city and the behaviour of its people, in Ayodhya, the issue of disputed kingship is resolved with grace and delicacy. Rama does not contest his father's decree that he be banished into the forest for fourteen years. His brother Bharata, who inherits the throne as a corollary to Rama's exile, is ashamed of his mother's machinations and tries to persuade Rama to take back the kingship which is rightfully his. He comes to meet Rama in Nandigram, where Rama has decided to live, and says,

> 'What will I do with this advice on the duties of a king when I have renounced kingship? ... The eternally established dharma states that while an older son lives, a younger son cannot be king. Come back with me to prosperous Ayodhya and crown yourself king for the glory of our clan!' (Sattar, chap. 25)

Rama refuses the throne and promises to reclaim his inheritance after he has lived out his fourteen years in the forest. The monkeys seem to live a more emotionally charged life in their city of Kishkindha than do the citizens of Ayodhya. As Sugriva tells Rama the story of his plight, he refers not only to Vali's power and strength but also to his love of sensuality and drink, of how Vali has claimed Sugriva's wife Ruma even as he reclaimed the kingdom. After Vali's death, Rama cannot enter the city of Kishkindha because of the terms of his exile. But Lakshmana enters Kishkindha after the rains have ended, to remind Sugriva, who has succumbed to the same love of luxury and pleasure as his brother, of his promise to help Rama rescue Sita.

Lakshmana looked around the city nestling in the valley with its jewel-studded buildings and flower-filled gardens. Full of elegant mansions and shops, Kishkindha overflowed with trees which flowered and fruited all through the year. The monkey citizens were the children of gods and gandharvas and they could change their forms at will. They were beautiful to behold in their fine clothes and celestial garlands. Kishkindha's roads were perfumed with flowers and sandal-paste and the fragrance of natural liquors like mead and toddy wafted through the air. Lakshmana saw the homes of the great monkey chiefs and the wide thoroughfares that gleamed like white clouds. They were decorated with celestial flowers, filled with wealth and grain and adorned by women who shone like jewels.

The king's palace rivalled Indra's. It was surrounded by sparkling white walls which were hard to breach. It had several white towers like the peaks of Mount Kailasha. Its garden had trees gifted by Indra that gave any kind of fruit that you could wish for. They were covered with flowers and provided generous, soothing shade.

Mighty Lakshmana entered Sugriva's palace uninvited, as the sun enters a huge cloud. He passed through seven courtyards before he came to the heavily guarded inner apartments which were filled with couches of gold and

> silver and seats covered with rich and beautiful brocades. Lakshmana could hear soft and melodious music as he walked in and he saw scores of women, all of them revelling in their youth and beauty. They sat there, adorned with rare flowers and exquisite jewels, weaving garlands. Lakshmana could not see a single retainer who was lazy, discontented or not fully adorned. (Sattar, chap. 40)

For all that Ayodhya is a city of restraint, Kishkindha seems to be a city of pleasure. The monkeys are honourable, but they are also good-looking hedonists who love silks and brocades and jewels and fine liquors. There is a lushness that hangs over Kishkindha and defines the actions of its citizens. The dharma of the monkeys permits the transfer of wives between brothers and monkey women appear to have freedoms that human women do not. While Tara and Ruma are Sugriva's wives, Tara is also a wise counsellor who advises her first husband Vali and then does the same for Sugriva when he takes her as his wife after Vali's death. She is also the one who explains to Lakshmana that Sugriva had not forgotten his promise to Rama, that he had merely lost himself in the pleasures that he had been denied for all his years in exile. It is as if she is making a case for Sugriva to recover himself as a pleasure-loving monkey before he can be of any real use to Rama.

The situation in Kishkindha presents us with an inverted mirror of what has happened in Ayodhya. Again, there are two brothers, one of whom is in exile, and there is only one throne. The Kishkindha dispute is resolved more aggressively, by the younger brother having the older brother killed. Further, Rama and Sugriva are united by the fact that their wives have been abducted. Both will get their wives back when the abductor has been killed. The grace of Ayodhya has been replaced with violence, with a more visceral solution that is in keeping with the heightened emotions that motivate the citizens of Kishkindha, whether it is Vali and his anger or Sugriva and his fear. Even Rama has one of his (few) explosions of rage here in Kishkindha when he believes that Sugriva has forgotten the terms of their alliance.

The Ramayana reserves its best for last with regard to the cities it describes. It is never more lyrical, never more astonishing in its visual imagery than when it describes Lanka, the island city of Ravana, where virtuous Sita has been imprisoned. Even Hanuman, citizen of Kishkindha where the liquor flows and there are silks and jewels everywhere, is astounded by what he sees in Ravana's city, and is so seduced by its beauty that he almost forgets why he is there.[13]

> Hanuman gazed in wonder at the city of Lanka which seemed like the city of the gods. It had beautiful golden

---

[13] Hanuman's adventures in Lanka are narrated in the Sundara Kanda, 'The Book of Beauty' or, more commonly, 'The Book Beautiful'. There has never been a completely satisfactory explanation for why this is the only book in the Ramayana that is named with an adjective/abstract noun when the other six are named for the temporal or spatial location of the action in the story. I would like to argue that this is the book in which the audience of the Ramayana, through the eyes of Hanuman, is witness to the beauty of Lanka, a beauty so magical and seductive, so utterly overwhelming, that it can be very dangerous.

> gateways and ramparts, with climbing vines carved on them, that surrounded hundreds of mansions festooned with flags and banners. Situated on top of a mountain, the city with its dazzling white buildings looked like it was hanging in the air ... Hanuman reached the northern gates and saw the city spread before him like a woman, the walls and ramparts her body, the vast ocean her clothes, the fortifications her hair and the upper storeys of the mansions her earrings. Lanka was as high and lofty as the peaks of Kailasha and seemed to touch the sky. Its tall buildings seemed poised to take off into the air. (Sattar, chap. 45)

What Hanuman sees when he enters the city is even more wondrous. His experience of Lanka is at night, not in darkness but bathed in a seductive and sympathetic moonlight.

> When night fell, he rose and entered the magnificent city which was divided into quarters by huge, wide roads. Its multi-storeyed mansions had floors of crystal set in gold and the mansions themselves were studded with pearls and gems ... Hanuman entered the city filled with lofty mansions that were like autumn clouds ... [he] climbed on to Lanka's ramparts which were made of precious metals, and stared in astonishment at the golden gates adorned with pearls and lapis and diamonds, decorated with beaten gold and silver. (Sattar, chaps. 45–46)

Hanuman enters Ravana's palace where

> there were thousands of golden vehicles and heavily carved palanquins that shone like the sun. There were vine-covered arbours, opulent rooms, picture galleries, recreation areas with hills fashioned out of wood, pleasant sitting rooms and lavish bedrooms. The palace shone like the sun because of its jewels and because of Ravana's own splendour. Flowing with honey and all kinds of liquor in jewelled vessels, it was like the palace of the god of wealth. (Sattar, chap. 46)

The opulence and excess of Lanka are mentioned over and over again, each image of sensuality and decadence outdoing the one before. And once again, as with Kishkindha, the essence of the city is located in the descriptions of its women.

> Hanuman saw exquisite women who appeared to be high-minded, virtuous and pure. They shone like stars, absorbed in their lovers and in drinking. He saw other women who were illuminated by their own beauty, but they were shy and hid in their lovers' arms, like birds clinging to their mates, enjoying a night of bliss ... He saw women with smooth complexions, bare-breasted, with skin the colour of molten gold, others with skin like moonlight ... Everywhere he looked, Hanuman saw rows upon rows of moon-bright faces, eyes with long, curling lashes and ornaments that glittered like garlands of lightning. (Sattar, chap. 46)

In Ravana's inner apartments, the beauty and sensuality of the women that Hanuman looks upon increases a thousandfold.

> There were women from the families of royal sages, daityas, gandharvas and rakshasas, and they had all come to Ravana out of love. None had been carried away against her will, they had all been won over by Ravana's personality. None had ever loved another or been the wife of another, none except Sita, the daughter of Janaka. Each of Ravana's wives was nobly born, beautiful, skilled in the arts of pleasure and extremely desirable. And the monkey, who had only worthy thoughts, said to himself, 'How lucky Rama would be if his wife was like the wives of this rakshasa king!' Then he grew agitated and reminded himself that Sita was far better than these other women and that the king of Lanka had done a terrible and ignoble thing. (Sattar, chap. 46)

Surely Lanka is Ayodhya turned around: fortified strength has become proud decoration, prosperity and wealth have become sensual beauty and showy ostentation, virtue has turned to passion, chastity and restraint into promiscuity and indulgence. These same qualities are displayed in the way Lanka's kingship is sorted out. Once again, Rama is the instrument by which a younger brother acquires a throne.[14]

---

[14] It is useful, also, to read these mirrored situations in the light of Rama's anxieties, all of which have been sublimated in the idealized world of Ayodhya: What if he has to fight Bharata for the throne when he returns from his exile (like Vali did and then Sugriva)? What if he had left Sita behind in the palace (like Ruma and Tara)? What is happening to her in her captivity? What are the consequences when a ruler allows love and desire to cloud his better judgement (like Dasharatha and Ravana)?

Vibhishana believes that Ravana is an unrighteous ruler and so, he leaves his brother and plots with Rama about how best to conquer Lanka and overcome the might of the rakshasas. Vibhishana's actions are duplicitous, reflecting the secrecy and shadows of the night. Ravana's enormous arrogance will not allow him to return Sita, nor will it let him admit to any mistakes that he might have made. Vibhishana does not fit in this atmosphere charged with excess and immoderation, a spectacular and uncaring decadence that can only be hurtling towards its own doom.

Hanuman's first vision of Lanka is as a woman. It is noteworthy that there are no physical descriptions of Ayodhya's women similar to those for the women of Kishkindha and Lanka. While we have some sense of what individual women (for example, Sita, Kaikeyi, Manthara and Kaushalya) are like, there are no descriptions of Ayodhya's women as a group at all. One could argue that the way women are portrayed is contiguous with the city and the culture/dharma that each of the cities supports. The conservative nature of human relations in Ayodhya is amplified by the fact that the city's women are not described in terms of their bodies and in relation to men. Ayodhya's women are chaste and submissive and stay well within their conjugal boundaries, which makes Manthara's conniving and Kaikeyi's petulant greed all the more remarkable. In Kishkindha, where monkey dharma allows shared sexual partners, women are described in some detail. And finally, in Lanka where rakshasa dharma allows multiple partners and even abductions, the women are lavishly and lovingly described in all their sensual glory.

Just as human, monkey and rakshasa women have different boundaries in terms of whom they can sleep with and how, so too, cities define the possible relations within themselves and offer different solutions to the problems of disputed kingship. It is as if the city is the boundary within which societies can flourish in their unique coherence and with a single dharma in operation, whether it is human society in Ayodhya, monkey society in Kishkindha or rakshasa society in Lanka. It is through these descriptions of the cities and the women that inhabit them that we see how clearly dharma, its maintenance as well as its violation, centres around women. More particularly, in the Ramayana, dharma hovers on the borders of conjugal behaviour and marital transgressions.

The forest (or rather, any space outside the city), on the other hand, is an indeterminate space where multiple dharmas can coexist, from the austerity of the sages to the excesses of Shurpanakha, for example. It is established as a space of fluidity, where shapes can change and where unusual and challenging choices become available. Many scholars have pointed to the fact that in literatures across the world, spaces outside the city are seen as liminal zones, places where transgressions can occur without retribution. The rules of the city do not apply, characters come up against the unexpected, the magical and the dangerous. I would like to extend this insight and suggest that when transgressive behaviours or acts (which might have been 'allowed' in the forests and in the wilderness) are committed within the city, it leads to disaster. A determined way of life is threatened and, quite often, shaken. These behaviours have to be contained or uprooted for order to be restored. In Indian texts, these violations and their repair can be read in terms of dharma and its imperatives.

In the case of the Ramayana, where we have already noted that dharma is created, maintained and violated primarily around women, the transgressions of this dharma within the city are indeed catastrophic. The nature and the severity of the violation are determined by the nature of dharma in each particular city but each of the violations involves a woman. Further, Dasharatha, Vali and Ravana all violate the conditions of their own dharma with these acts. Dasharatha's surrender to Kaikeyi's demands goes against the dharma established in Ayodhya, where the norms of behaviour are about restraint and the public good. Vali's addition of Ruma to his harem within the walls of Kishkindha while Sugriva is still alive violates the dharma of Kishkindha which is otherwise rather more permissive with regard to multiple wives and female partners. And so, too, with Ravana – he brings Sita to Lanka by force whereas all the other hundreds of women in his palace have come to him out of their own choice. Any of these actions, from Dasharatha or Vali or Ravana, might have been permissible in the space outside the city, but once they occur within the city, they become transgressive violations.

What, then, about the dharma that controls the behaviour and emotions of the women themselves around whom these violations revolve? Once again, we see that each city and each space has a different set of conditions. The women of Ayodhya are chaste, bound by and respectful of their conjugal vows, fundamentally submissive, particularly in terms of their sexual powers and desires. Sita would epitomize this dharma and Kaikeyi would be the violator thereof. In Kishkindha, despite the air of smouldering promiscuity, the queens, Tara and Ruma, are allowed to belong to more than one male but apparently only after they have been widowed. Tara becomes loyal to Sugriva only after Vali's death. In Lanka, Mandodari is Ravana's chief queen, but other rakshasa women have lovers. Moreover, Ravana's inner apartments are filled with non-rakshasa women who have chosen to be there out of their desire for him, suggesting that they, like common rakshasa women, are permitted to exercise sexual choice. Just as Kaikeyi does not 'fit' in Ayodhya with her naked ambition and her manipulation of her aged husband, so also Sita's blazing chastity is equally a disturbance in the city of the rakshasas.

While cities can accommodate only one dharma at a time, once again, the forest becomes a space where multiple dharmas can and do exist simultaneously for women as well. We know that the sages' wives inhabit the forest with their firm adherence to the rules and regulations of marriage and hermitage living. When Shurpanakha approaches Rama and Lakshmana in the Dandaka forest, she says, 'I am the rakshasi Shurpanakha and I can change my form at will. I do as I please. I wander through this forest by myself and I strike terror into the hearts of all creatures.' She describes her rakshasa brothers and ends her introduction with the boast about her freedom as a single woman that 'none of them have any control over me' (Sattar, chap. 29).[15] In direct contrast to Shurpanakha and all that her presence in the forest

---

[15] Katherine Erndl has already noted that Shurpanakha personifies the forest and that she shares the characteristics of the wild, untamed and, therefore, dangerous space that she inhabits. Erndl also makes reference

implies, there is also the mysterious Swayamprabha, the self-illuminated ascetic who lives in an enchanted cave into which the monkeys stumble as they search for Sita. Swayamprabha saves the monkey army and transports them directly to the shores of the ocean through the power of her austerities. The forest, therefore, supports the excess and indulgence of Shurpanakha as well as the fierce celibacy of Swayamprabha.

While it would appear that human dharma is one among many possible dharmas (and monkeys and rakshasas seem to believe that it is simply that, continuing to live within the boundaries of their own codes), Rama says something different. Vali, the rightful king of Kishkindha, is killed by Rama for a violation of a specific dharma which does not permit taking another man's wife, despite the fact that the practice is sanctioned among the monkeys. Rama says to the dying Vali,

> 'Here is the first reason for my killing you. You have rejected the eternal dharma and slept with your brother's wife. You lust for Ruma and sleep with her even though Sugriva is still alive. This is unacceptable because you should treat her as a daughter-in-law. I killed you for sleeping with your brother's wife and because you were motivated by lust! There can be no other punishment for this violation of dharma and of the worldly code. The man who sleeps with his sister, his daughter or his brother's wife

---

to the idea that Shurpanakha is the complete opposite of Sita who embodies the controlled and orderly nature of the city.

> is punished by death according to the traditional texts.' (Sattar, chap. 38)

Rama's killing of Ravana comes from the same motivation, the transgressive act of taking the wife of another man. Of course, in this case, the situation is rather more personal as the wife in question is Rama's. No matter that rakshasa dharma permits the abduction of women, like Vali, Ravana is judged by Rama's yardstick and found wanting. Rama's actions and reactions with regard to both Vali and Ravana seem to imply that whatever the dharma of a city and its citizens, the dharma of a king is different and above all other dharmas. Unlike his father, Rama upholds the impossible dictates of a kingly dharma when he banishes his own beloved wife because of market gossip about her chastity.

Apart from all this, Rama seems to be searching for something else, an 'eternal dharma'[16] that would be universal rather than specific to time and place and order of being, a code that would explain and justify all that has been done to him and his reactions to it – his father's decree by which he loses his kingdom and is banished into the forest, his wife's abduction, the fact that his fate pulls him back into the role of a kshatriya that he has tried so hard to resist. What could possibly make all this reasonable? And bearable? In the quiet of the forest and under the benign influence of the sages, Rama seeks the answers to the big

---

[16] However, Bharata also makes reference to this 'eternal dharma' when he asks Rama to take back the kingdom. In his case, eternal dharma refers to the fact that a younger brother cannot be king as long as the older brother is alive.

questions of his life. He needs to understand what logic allowed his father to give precedence to the personal promises he had made to his wife, promises that overrode his duties as a king. He also needs to know that obeying his father's wishes as he did was worth something – otherwise his obedience remains a vainglorious gesture that results in more and more personal anguish. What could justify the abduction of his gentle, innocent wife? Could it be because of his own actions – the humiliation of Shurpanakha and the pledge to protect the forest sages from the rakshasas – that Ravana's passions were incited? What gave him the right to pursue an enmity with the rakshasas that was not his? And what moral code allowed him to attack a defenceless woman whose only crime was sexual aggression?[17]

As Rama questions the code by which he has lived thus far and thinks about the rightness of his own emotions and deeds, he begins to question the codes that others live by as well – his illustrious father, Vali and Ravana. As his own dharma – his sense of the world and his place in it – from which he acts, proves to be inadequate, so too, the ethical bases for the actions of those like him (Vali and Ravana) also appear wanting. His quest for an eternal dharma becomes more urgent. He seeks not simply a dharma that will answer all his questions but a dharma that will allow him to live and act in the world such that he betrays neither his past nor his future. Can one be a righteous king without resorting to violence, for example?

---

[17] What he learned from Vishvamitra in the incident with Tataka was precisely this: that rakshasis and yakshis were to be maimed and mutilated, if not killed outright.

Once again, however, Rama's ambitions for himself remain unrealized. All his attempts to change, to adopt the gentle and unobtrusive life of an ascetic (where perhaps the 'eternal dharma' can be lived), come to naught when Sita is abducted.[18] It is this, and not the banishment, that is the life-changing moment for Rama. He can no longer afford to understand why others do what they do and what might justify their actions. The quest for the eternal dharma has ended and Rama slides back into the dharma that he was born into, that of a righteous warrior with the licence to live by and provoke violence.

From this point onwards, because of the intensity of his anguish, Rama has only one idea that drives him – there can be no dharma that justifies the taking of another man's wife. In that sense, he has returned to the idea of a universal dharma, one that stands in all circumstances and in all times. The problem that remains is why Rama takes on the enforcement of that dharma. What empowers him to punish those who violate it? Of course, if Rama is god, he must ensure that this dharma prevails in the world. But as a human hero, what gives him the right to kill Vali and Ravana? Could it be that, like his father, he too, finally, has made an error of judgement because of his love for a woman? That his grief at losing his wife has enraged him to the point of irrationality? Rama kills Ravana because Ravana has taken Sita,

---

[18] Several times in the forest, Rama says that a life based in dharma is far superior to one that is motivated by artha and kama, that wealth and pleasure cannot be the bases for acting in the world. As he questions his own actions, he sees that the actions of others that cause the most damage are motivated by pleasure, whether it is Dasharatha's decree or Vali's and Ravana's actions.

but he kills Vali simply because he is blinded by a misplaced rage.

We know that once Sita has been taken from him, Rama's anger returns. Earlier too, the first time we see Rama's anger is when Viradha picks up Sita and places her on his hip.

> Rama's eyes blazed with anger as he shouted back at the rakshasa who had bloodshot eyes and wicked intentions. 'Shame on you for your base motives! You are obviously seeking death. Stand and fight with me and you shall certainly find it!' Rama fitted his straightest and sharpest arrows into his bow. Seven gold-tipped arrows blazed like tongues of flame as they flew with the speed of the wind, resounding through the air. (Sattar, chap. 28)

Rama is enraged when he believes that Sugriva has forgotten his promise to help find Sita. Rama says to Lakshmana,

> 'Go to Kishkindha and find that idiot king of the monkeys! Give him this message from me ... "Obviously, you want to see me draw my bow, decorated with gold, that flashes like lightning on the battlefield. You wish to hear again the thunderous resonance of my bowstring as I draw it back in anger!" ... Go to Sugriva and tell him how angry I am! Tell him also, "The road that Vali took is not yet closed! Stick to your commitment, Sugriva, and do not follow Vali down that path! I killed Vali with a single arrow. I can also kill you and your entire family!"' (Sattar, chap. 39)

Rama is also willing to take on the mighty ocean when he realizes that the ocean is the last obstacle to reaching Lanka where his beloved is imprisoned. As he sits by the ocean waiting for the god of the waters to appear, he gets more and more angry.

> Rama's eyes turned red with anger and he said to Lakshmana, '... the virtues of good men, like calmness, patience, honesty and sweet speech bear no results. They are seen as signs of weakness ... One cannot achieve fame and success in this world without violence, just as one cannot achieve victory in battle without it ... Today I shall declare war on this mighty ocean, filled with shells and fish, and I shall dry up his waters! ... Bring me my bow, Lakshmana, and my arrows which are like poisonous snakes ...' His eyes dilated with anger, Rama grabbed his bow and he blazed like the doomsday fire. (Sattar, chap. 57)

The gentle Rama of the forest, the one who renounced kshatriya dharma because it was violent, has returned to violence in order to get his wife back. Anything and anyone that stands in the way of that goal will bear the brunt of his anger – Vali, the ocean, Ravana. Sadly for Rama, despite all his efforts, he has fallen prey to the same failing as his father. Dasharatha's love for Kaikeyi impelled him to act unjustly towards his oldest son and his people. Rama's love for Sita has led him down the road to unrighteous violence. This becomes all the more ironic because it was Sita who pleaded with Rama in the forest to give up his weapons as their presence alone would attract violence. After the encounter with Viradha (which is a sign of things to come – more attacks by rakshasas as well as her abduction), Sita says to Rama,

> 'But the third weakness[19] which men succumb to because of their passions, the inflicting of violence and cruelty upon other beings without reason or enmity, that weakness appears to be present in you now ... Now that you are here with your brother and you are both armed, you shall see many forest creatures. Inevitably, you will be tempted to use your arrows. Like dry fuel bursts into flame when it is near a fire, so too, a kshatriya's passions are ignited when he has a bow at hand ... What a difference there is ... between the vows of a kshatriya and those of an ascetic! We must learn to respect the code of behaviour of the world we now inhabit. Here, the mind is perverted by extreme proximity to weapons. You can return to the code of the kshatriyas when we go back to Ayodhya!
>
> 'But if you were to give up the kingdom entirely and embrace the life of an ascetic, I am sure that my parents-in-law would be very happy. Everything in this world, including wealth and happiness, come from dharma. There is nothing greater than dharma.' (Sattar, chap. 28)

Sita echoes what Rama has already tentatively attempted and expressed once they leave the city. This makes him firmer in his resolve to follow the ascetics' code and seek dharma rather

[19] It would be remiss not to mention that one of the weaknesses that Sita lists in this long speech is lusting after the wife of another man.

than wealth and pleasure. Once again, it is in the forest, that fluid space where many dharmas are possible, that Rama can attempt to be someone else, follow a path other than the one into which he has been born. Within a city, there are no choices, but the forest/wilderness offers a respite from this determined universe, however hard it may be to change one's habits and break with past behaviours. With Sita, his beloved as well as his inspiration, gone, Rama can no longer stay this difficult course of renunciation and change. He succumbs to the very weakness that Sita cautions him against – the lure of violence without reason and enmity. Even before he returns to Ayodhya, where it would be appropriate for him to take on his kshatriya role again, as Sita says, Rama has turned his back on his ascetic vows.[20]

Rama's only chance to change himself lies outside the city. He knows that when he returns to the city, he will have to revert to the dharma that Ayodhya demands and supports, for the vows of an ascetic and the eternal dharma will not be appropriate there. The idyllic freedom of the forest, the hope and the love, will have passed into memory, all the more painful because when Sita leaves Rama for the final time, she will take with her the fact as well as the hope of a different life for them both.

---

[20] It is also remarkable that Sita says that even if Rama were to live by his ascetic vows for longer than his time in the forest, his parents would not be upset. She, too, carries the pain of Dasharatha's lapse and wants her husband to rise above the possibility of that kind of error.

LOST LOVES

Valmiki's Ramayana opens with the incident of one of a pair of krauncha birds being killed by a hunter. Valmiki is so moved by the surviving bird's grief that he expresses his empathy for the birds, so cruelly separated, in a new metre, which is then explored and perfected as it is used to tell the story of Rama. But we have other reasons to take note of the bird's death. A.K. Ramanujan, in his seminal essay, 'Three Hundred Ramayanas: Five Examples and Three Thoughts on Translation', writes about the moment when Valmiki expresses his grief in the new metre and remarks on it as an example of bhava becoming rasa, a feeling that is transformed into an aesthetic emotion. Ramanujan also indicates to us that each of the two endings for the story – the happy reunion followed by the return to Ayodhya, and Sita's second abandonment and eventual departure – creates a different mood for the story as a whole. The second one, the tragic ending, makes the story one of vipralambha, of separated lovers. I would like to combine these insights and suggest that since the loving birds are separated by the death of one and the surviving bird's grief moves Valmiki, it is this same emotion (that of separated lovers) that has to remain with us when Valmiki's story is over. Because Valmiki's connection with telling Rama's story is located in the moment of the bird's grief at losing her beloved, the Rama story that Valmiki tells will mirror the same emotion and end with separation and loss rather than union and joy.

It is almost as if the leitmotif of Valmiki's Ramayana is separation. Children are separated from their parents, brothers from brothers, wives from husbands. Most often, these separations are caused by death (for example, the widows of all the brave kings such as Dasharatha's wives, as well as Mandodari and Tara; and the separation between brothers like Vali and Sugriva, and Ravana and Vibhishana), but not only and always so. Before Dasharatha dies, he is separated from two of his sons. Just as Vali and Sugriva are apart before Vali's death, Rama leaves his mother and his other two brothers behind when he goes into exile, as does Lakshmana, who is even separated from his twin brother Shatrughna.[21] Many of these separations are occasioned by curses, and the Ahalya story in the Bala Kanda gives us a clue as to the mood of the text, for she too is separated from her husband Gautama, also because of a curse.

But it is the separation between Rama and Sita that most moves us, partly because they are the central characters in the story, but also because it is a separation that is created by circumstance (Sita's abduction) and then perpetuated (or repeated) by choices that Rama and Sita make. For all that the Ramayana is about righteous and rightful kingship and the battle between two equally matched protagonists, one 'good' and the other not quite so, it is also a love story, albeit one that is full

[21] In some versions of the Rama story, Lakshmana is also separated from his wife Urmila when he chooses to go into the forest with Rama and Sita.

of pain and sorrow. It is about loving someone and then losing them, and about learning to live with the loss of love.

Sita and Rama begin their lives together in the palace, surrounded by retainers and committed to their various royal duties. In Valmiki's Ramayana, we are never quite sure how old they are when their conventional lives as king and queen in waiting are shattered by Kaikeyi's cruel demands.[22] But there is little doubt that they are young people, perhaps in their early twenties. When Hanuman finds Sita in the ashoka grove in Lanka and convinces her that he is a messenger from Rama, she tells him about her life before the period of exile.

> 'I am Sita, the wife of Rama! For twelve full years I lived in Rama's palace, enjoying all the pleasures known to humans and satisfying my every desire. Then, in the thirteenth year, the king and his ministers decided to consecrate Rama heir and when everything was ready for the ceremony, the lady Kaikeyi spoke to her husband ...' (Sattar, chap. 50)

In any event, these protected young people are catapulted into an unfamiliar world that is unpredictable and dangerous. Along with Lakshmana, they embark on their new lives with fortitude and determination. But while life in the forest is hard and they are compelled to move from place to place, this is the time

[22] The larger tradition is clear that Rama and Sita were married at sixteen. In the Bala Kanda, when Vishvamitra comes to take Rama away to fight Tataka, Dasharatha pleads with the sage, saying that his son is too young, 'My lotus-eyed Rama is only fifteen years old. I don't think he can face the rakshasas in battle!' (Sattar, chap. 5).

when Rama and Sita can grow into their relationship with each other, sheltered by Lakshmana and far away from their public lives and duties. Sita is delighted by the flowers and the forest animals that soon become her pets and she revels in small acts of domesticity. Rama, too, puts aside his kshatriya codes of behaviour and is able to live a quiet life of contemplation. In this idyll, despite the discomfort and the looming threats from the rakshasas, their feelings for each other mature and their love blooms as they pass into adulthood.

When Hanuman finds Sita in the ashoka grove, she recalls for him an incident from her time in the forest that says much about her relationship with Rama. Once, Sita and Rama were enjoying an intimate moment together when a crow swooped down from the sky and attacked Sita, eventually pecking her on her breast. Enraged, Rama took a blade of grass and invoked Brahma's weapon. The blade of grass chased the crow all through the three worlds as it tried to escape. The crow finally came back to Rama for refuge, but since Rama had already empowered the blade of grass and could not recall the divine weapon, he injured the crow's right eye but saved his life. We also know how protective Rama is about his gentle wife when Viradha snatches her up. He says to Lakshmana,

> 'This beautiful princess, the delicate daughter of Janaka and my lovely wife, who has been reared with every comfort imaginable, is being forced to sit on Viradha's hip ... I cannot bear the thought of Sita being touched by another man. It upsets me more than the death of my father and the loss of my kingdom!' (Sattar, chap. 28)

And again, when Shurpanakha appears and attempts to seduce the brothers, Rama is patient with her until the moment she lunges for Sita. All humour gone, Rama berates Lakshmana for teasing the rakshasi and stands by as Lakshmana cuts off her nose and ears.

Rama is utterly distraught when he comes back from chasing the magical deer and finds Sita missing.

> But though he searched high and low, Rama could not find his beloved in the forest. His eyes red from weeping, he seemed like a madman as he ran from tree to tree, from the mountains to the river, weeping more and more as he plunged deeper and deeper into an ocean of grief … Rama called out as he ran hither and thither in the forest. He leapt and jumped and spun around as if he were crazy. He could not stand still for a moment, so he ran through the forests, over the mountains and down to the streams and rivers. (Sattar, chap. 34)

Finally, with a lot of help from Lakshmana, Rama calms down and thinks about how to rescue Sita. As they wait for the rainy season to end and for the great monkey army to gather,

> Rama was not happy. He thought constantly about his abducted wife who was dearer to him than life. He would lie down every night, but the beauty of his surroundings made it impossible for him to sleep. Never really free from sadness, Rama would find his eyes brimming with tears at times like this. (Sattar, chap. 39)

Meanwhile, in her captivity, Sita has grown wan and pale as she pines for her beloved Rama. She thinks of him constantly, holding him in her heart, and she begs Hanuman to tell Rama to rescue her, to tell him how she cannot live without him.

> 'Have pity on me and make sure that I am reunited as soon as possible with Rama. I yearn for him so! Remind him of the blade of grass he sent after the crow that put out one of his eyes. Tell him to remember the vermilion he smeared on my cheek when the one on my forehead had been wiped off! ... Tell him, "I have treasured and protected this jewel, born from the sea, that I am sending you now. I would look at it and think that I was looking at your face and it would make me happy! I cannot live like this for much longer ... I will hold on for another month, but after that, I cannot be separated from you, great prince!"' (Sattar, chap. 50)

It is very touching that the stories Sita tells Hanuman about Rama are ones of great tenderness, for these are surely the intimate moments she recalls most often in her time away from him. And though she speaks often of his valour and courage, her private thoughts lie with Rama her lover and beloved and not with the warrior prince who will rescue her against all odds.

Hanuman sets Lanka on fire and returns to the monkeys in triumph. He tells them about his adventures crossing the ocean and describes meeting Sita.

> 'But now, that good woman sits miserably under a tree in Ravana's grove. Surrounded by cruel rakshasis, she is

> emaciated and tormented by grief, lustreless as the moon hidden by clouds. She is devoted to her marital vows and stands firm in her dharma. She is not in the least interested in the arrogant Ravana. She thinks of nothing but Rama all the time, with her whole heart.' (Sattar, chap. 53)

Again, we are never sure in Valmiki's Ramayana when Sita was abducted in terms of the fourteen years in the forest or how long she was in captivity and away from Rama. We do know that the end of the war and, therefore, the end of their separation, coincides with the end of the period of exile, for Rama and Sita return to Ayodhya after Ravana has been killed. We can assume that Sita is in captivity for at least a few months, as Rama has to wait for the rains to end before the search for Sita can begin. But we get the feeling that her time away from Rama is much longer, perhaps because when we are with Sita we absorb her feeling of how interminable this period is. There is nothing she can do, other than hope to be rescued as she wards off Ravana's attempts to seduce her and stands firm against his threats to kill her. She keeps her mind and heart fixed on Rama as she tries to remain strong and believe in the possibility of being saved.

Rama, on the other hand, has had much to do after Sita has been taken from him. And it is in this period that he realizes he cannot escape his destiny as a warrior and a king. The time in the forest, with and without Sita, has been one of profound change for Rama. He starts by treating the time in exile as an opportunity to reconsider the values he was brought up with. Profoundly shocked by his father's inability to do the 'right' thing, he is exposed to the quietude of the sages at this vulnerable time in his life. Contemplation rather than action seems attractive to Rama and he renounces a dharma of violence and anger as he seeks a new way to be in the world. Even as he learns to control his more volatile emotions, Sita is abducted. Rama finds that he needs to retrieve all that he has rejected – the anger that will let him kill those that stand in the way of rescuing his wife and the martial skills he had set aside all these years. Additionally and also under the influence of the forest sages, Rama resolves to slowly withdraw from the love he feels for Sita, for he knows that there will be a terrible moment of truth when he will have to ask his abducted wife for proof of her chastity. This premonition comes from the fact that he has already decided that he will not be judged for the same fault as his father – of being blinded by love for a woman.

The combination of Rama returning to his kshatriya dharma and simultaneously distancing himself emotionally from Sita is what causes the biggest rupture in their relationship. During their early days in the forest, Sita had spoken passionately to Rama about renouncing violence, an idea that he had already entertained when he spoke of rejecting the dharma of a kshatriya. Sita grows to love her gentle, contemplative husband who increasingly hands over his warrior duties to his brother. It is Lakshmana who kills the animals for their food and Lakshmana who mutilates Shurpanakha. In the earlier encounter with Viradha, when Rama breaks into tears at the sight of his wife held by another man, Lakshmana explodes into anger and reminds Rama that he should be enraged at this violation. Rama then finds the anger within himself and attacks and kills Viradha. Rama needs to recall the emotions and the actions he had handed over to Lakshmana in the months of waiting as he prepares to rescue his wife.

All the encounters with sundry attackers and rakshasas that precede the final confrontation with Ravana are merely preparations, tests along the way to keep Rama's skills intact. The battle with Ravana is the last but inevitable step that Rama takes out of his hard-won private life and into the public destiny of kingship that he thought he could escape in the forest.

Despite his paralysing grief at Sita's abduction, Rama realizes that he needs to restrain his love for Sita, to control it such that it does not overwhelm and weaken him. He knows he will win her back but he also knows that to be queen, to share his public destiny, she will have to bear the humiliation of a public test of her chastity. He hardens his heart towards her so that he will be capable of the harshness and terrible cruelty he has to display at the moment of their reunion.

For all that Rama reluctantly takes on his kshatriya role again, he does so fully, burying his other self deep within. When Sita sees him at the end of the war and hears what he has to say to her, she is appalled. Behind the hardened warrior that stands before her, resolute in his harsh words and deeds, she searches for her gentle husband, the man who taught her the names of the birds and trees in the forest, the tender lover who gathered flowers for her hair. That Rama is no longer visible, swallowed up by the long period of separation, remade in the mould of the king that he must be. As much as Rama may regret all that he has to say and do at this point and as much as his heart breaks (as we see from his tears and discomfort before he sees Sita at the end of the battle), it is Sita who has lost her love. She cannot recognize the man she faces, the man who has asked her to appear in public for the moment of their reunion, the man who has just told her that he has no use for her any more.[23]

After their reconciliation, which is facilitated by the gods, Sita returns to Ayodhya with Rama and their life together resumes, albeit under the shadow of their separation and within Rama's new role as king.

When Sita is banished and goes into the forest for the second time, she weeps piteously when she is abandoned by Lakshmana. She laments her situation and questions what she could possibly have done to deserve this treatment, and then she says to Lakshmana, 'Tell the king, "Always treat your subjects as you would your own brothers. That is the highest dharma and it will earn you incomparable fame and glory. I care nothing for this corporeal body of mine! You should do whatever it takes to prevent the people from gossiping!"' (Sattar, chap. 69). It would be easy to read this message to the king as the words of a good wife who places her husband and his dilemmas before everything else. But it's also possible to detect a trace of sarcasm in the last sentence and hear these words as Sita's resigned acceptance of the fact that Rama is now irrevocably and forever the king, a public person with a public life and public demands – choices that he has made for himself. The loving husband, Prince Rama of the forest, whom she searched for on the battlefield

[23] It would be interesting, also, to view Sita's evocation of the imagery of sati when she asks Lakshmana to build a fire for her test of chastity. The resonance with widowhood is strong if we think about the death of her beloved husband, the gentle, tender man of the forest.

has disappeared forever. In his place is Ramachandra, the king of Ayodhya.

This message to the king is when Sita conclusively renounces her love for Rama. From that moment at the end of the war, when she saw Rama, the full-blooded kshatriya, before her, she knew that he had changed. After the return to Ayodhya, she realizes that the man who had been the object of her great love, the love that had sustained her through the terrible loneliness and uncertainty of captivity, no longer existed. Once Sita relinquishes her love for Rama, she is able to make the momentous decision to leave him forever. She lives her life in the forest with her sons under the protection of Valmiki, reconciled to the fact that, while her sons might be reunited with their father, she will never be with Rama again. When Rama recognizes his sons at the sacrifice through listening to his own story, he asks for Sita to be brought before him for one last public trial that will prove her chastity. Sita comes to the sacrificial enclosure for another moment of reconciliation and reunion that is played out in public. Without a word to Rama or even a glance in his direction, she calls upon the earth to bear witness to her fidelity. Her invocation is loaded: 'If I have never thought about any other man but Rama, let the goddess Madhavi create a chasm for me!' (Sattar, chap. 70). The condition is quite simple – she is not asking to be proven innocent so that she can stay with Rama, rather, she asks that the consequence of her chastity be that she be taken away. Taken away from Rama and from any possibility of a life as his queen.

Sita finds it in herself to leave Rama because she has ceased to love him. More accurately, she cannot love the man that

Rama has chosen to become, whether it is because he has embraced the violence she begged him to reject when they were in the forest, or because he has placed his public honour before his personal truth, or because his honour and his truth have become one and the same thing. Perhaps the love he had for her has itself changed – it has become the love a king has for his consort rather than the transformative love that two human beings can have for each other. Sita sustained herself through her captivity by keeping her mind on Rama, holding close the idea of the man she loved and who loved her, a love that fed on separation as much as it was nourished by togetherness. Sita had to remain constant, but Rama's experiences demanded that he cast aside his new ideas and hopes and forge a self that would be up to the challenges before him. The Rama that Sita meets at the end of the war is not the man whom she had stored in her heart. Her idea of Rama, so carefully nurtured and cherished during their first separation, did not match the reality she was now faced with. At the second reunion, she makes the choice to leave him, a choice made somewhat easier by the fact that she is leaving not the man she loved, but the king of Kosala, the ruler of Ayodhya.

We are used to thinking of Sita as someone who deserves our pity and sympathy, a woman buffeted by the storms of circumstance – first, the innocent object of Ravana's desire, then, the equally innocent victim of her royal husband's honour and, ultimately, the abandoned wife. What we fail to see is Sita's courage and defiance in her final act on earth when she refuses to live with a continuing falsehood. It could be that she held her dreams too closely, that she did not grow into the life that lay ahead of her as she proved unwilling to bow to the dictates of being Rama's queen. Perhaps she could have done more to understand the man she had loved so wholeheartedly, who surely deserved more than that final disdainful dismissal. But the Ramayana is a story about love – how it can sustain us, how it must live in the shadow of public lives and commitments, how it can become the basis of personal truths that need to be lived out. While Rama chooses to place his love in the penumbra of his luminous public life, Sita chooses to place her love squarely in the glare of Rama's shining glory. As it turns out, neither the shadowed love nor the illuminated one is able to survive.

The tragedy of the Ramayana is not simply that there is no happy ending with Rama and Sita finally reunited. Sita disappears into the earth and Rama is left to his private grief in the company of his young sons. The greater tragedy is the death of their love for each other, which cannot renew itself in the changed (albeit for the better) circumstances of their lives. For all that Rama may still feel for his gentle wife, he cannot or will not express those feelings after the war and their return to Ayodhya. For all that Sita has loved her husband during the trials and tribulations of the exile, that love cannot sustain itself when Rama banishes her to the forest for a second time.

Sita's heartbroken departure can be seen as a rejection of a life made less by the absence of love, as an act of personal truth and public courage. Rama is left with a public truth and little else.

> When the sacrifice was over, Rama was very depressed that Sita was no longer with him. The entire world seemed

> empty to him and, overcome by his grief, he knew no peace of mind. He rewarded the brahmins suitably and sent them away along with the kings, the rakshasas and the monkeys. When they had all left, he went back to Ayodhya, carrying Sita in his heart.
>
> He did not marry again, and for every sacrifice after that, he placed a golden statue of Sita by his side. (Sattar, chap. 70)

Rama is left to live with his loss, boldly represented by the golden statue, a constant reminder to himself and his people of what he has sacrificed for the public good.

INSIDE/OUTSIDE

WHERE IS VALMIKI IN THE STORY THAT HE TELLS?

This essay is an attempt to understand the position of Valmiki in the Sanskrit Ramayana, an epic tale which he tells and in which he participates. He participates in the Ramayana as a teller of the tale (through a framed narrative) as well as a character who plays a crucial part in the denouement by taking care of Sita in her abandonment and helping to bring up her sons.[24]

After acknowledging the traditional (genre) distinction between the 'shruti' or 'revealed' and the 'smriti' or 'remembered' literatures, we need to contend with the 'authorship' of stories and literary materials in Sanskrit. It is with the so-called Indian epics that, for the first time, really, we have massive literary compositions that are attributed to single minds, to Valmiki for the Ramayana and to Vyasa for the Mahabharata.[25] Obviously, here we are not dealing with modern

---

[24] Earlier versions of this essay were delivered as papers at the R.K. Narayan Birth Centenary Conference, Mysore, October 2006, and at the Sahitya Akademi conference, 'The Image of the Writer in Indian Literature', Pune, February 2007. Another version of this essay appears in a festschrift volume for Wendy Doniger (Patton 2010).

[25] We believe the epics as we have them now were composed sometime between 200 BCE and 200 CE. But we are equally aware that some versions of the stories they tell were around for much longer.

notions of authorship and it could be further argued that we are dealing here with specifically, but not necessarily uniquely, Indian notions of authorship. Valmiki shows us that the author's participation in the story is the motivation for the telling of the story itself. Inspiration for telling does not exist solely outside the telling of the story but, more compellingly, *within* the story. Indeed, in order to tell it the author must be a witness and motivator of other characters – not simply a receiver of the story who happens to be 'in it' every once in a while.

The names of our epic authors are provided with significant etymologies and meanings: the name Valmiki is said to be derived from the Sanskrit word 'valmik', meaning 'anthill', a reference to one of the extra-textual biographies of the sage. So also, with Vyasa: the name is derived from the Sanskrit root 'vi', which means 'to divide/arrange/compile', which is extrapolated into the myth that Vyasa was the divinely endowed sage who divided the Vedas into four and then composed the Mahabharata. But consensus will allow 'Vyasa' to also mean 'the compiler', which suits more realistic notions of how the Mahabharata came to be this enormous text that includes a compelling narrative, some of the most unforgettable moments in literature, as well as discourses on dharma.

There is much debate about whether or not the composers of the Sanskrit epics were historical figures, as each comes to us with his own larger-than-life story. Sometimes, as in the case of Valmiki, they come to us with more than one story of who they are and how they came to be telling the tale that is now before us. The story of Valmiki within the Ramayana is quite simply that he was a sage who lived in the forest, and when he asked who the most perfect man was, Narada recited Rama's story to him. Outside the Ramayana, we have the story of the repentant brigand who became Valmiki through his devotion to Rama, so immersed in repeating the holy name that an anthill formed around him. His unflinching devotion and his meditation allowed him to then tell the wondrous tale of Rama, the best of men, and his actions. The latter story of the reformed brigand is known all over India and does not really contradict the story of Valmiki within the Ramayana itself. The same brigand could well have been transformed into the sage who asks the question, hears and then retells the story of Rama.

There is less doubt about the historicity of the composers of later Rama stories in other Indian languages, for example, about Kamban, Krittibasa or Tulsidas. But here too, historical fact and devotional certitude collide. While we know that Tulsidas and Kamban and other tellers of Rama's story existed as humans in a time that is historically counted in the same way as ours, we also know that there are elements in their biographies that stretch the credulity of the critical imagination in ways that do not challenge the more loving acceptance of divine grace by devotees.[26] Even as we accept that they are historical figures, we are also asked to contend with the Rama-related miracles in their lives and view their compositions through the lens of these unusual events and

[26] For example, we know that Tulsidas lived during the reign of the Mughal emperor Akbar and that he composed the *Ramcharitmanas* among other devotional texts. But his biography also contains stories about his encounters with Rama and Hanuman, which cannot be accorded the same truth status as the dates for his birth and death.

literary inspirations. It is important within traditional and critical scholarship about the epics that we know these extra-textual facts and constructed etymologies about Valmiki and Vyasa and other tellers of Rama's story, for they impinge on the way we receive the stories they tell us. If Valmiki is named for the anthill that covered him while he was deeply immersed in his thoughts of Rama after having been a brigand who was redeemed by the recitation of the holy name, then outside his Ramayana he is a bhakta, though the depth of that fervour might not be reflected in the story he tells.

Valmiki's 'authorship' of the Ramayana is complex and layered. His presence in the story of Rama occurs within the first and the last books of the Sanskrit epic, the Bala Kanda and the Uttara Kanda. At the start of the Sanskrit text (which might be usefully distinguished from the 'beginning of the story'), Narada tells Valmiki about Rama, the most perfect man in the world of humans.

> One day, [Valmiki] said to the eloquent Narada, 'Tell me, great one, who is the most virtuous man in the world of humans?' Narada, who knows the past, the present and the future, was delighted with Valmiki's question ... 'There is one man, O sage, who has all these virtues. Listen, and I will tell you about him ... Born into the clan of Ikshvaku, his name is Rama.' (Sattar, chap. 1)

Narada then tells Valmiki the story of Rama from the moment his coronation was announced to his triumphal return to Ayodhya followed by his long and righteous reign as king.

Some time later, Valmiki sees a hunter kill one of a pair of mating birds and the grief of the surviving bird moves Valmiki to such an extent that he expresses his sympathy in a new poetic metre.

> Compassion welled up in Valmiki's heart when he saw the fallen bird, killed so unrighteously, and the grief of its mate. Deeply moved, he said, 'Hunter, because you killed this bird while he was making love, you shall never find a resting place!'
>
> As soon as he had spoken, Valmiki thought to himself, 'What are these words that I uttered in my grief for the bird?' Learned and wise, the sage said to his disciple, 'My words came forth in a metre of four feet with equal syllables that can be sung to the notes of the veena. Since this metre arose from my grief, let it henceforth be known as the shloka metre!' Bharadvaja committed the new metre uttered by his teacher to memory and Valmiki was deeply satisfied. (Sattar, chap. 2)

After this, Valmiki performs his customary rituals and then passes into a meditative trance. Brahma appears before him, but Valmiki remains distracted and distressed by what he has just witnessed, that is, the killing of the bird. He recites the new metre for Brahma, and Brahma smiles and says,

> 'Your mind did not create this shloka metre. I produced this eloquence in you. O best of all sages, use this new metre to recite the tale of Rama … as you heard it told by Narada …

> Recite the acts of Sita, the known ones and the unknown ones. Whatever you do not know will become known to you. It will prevail on earth as long as the mountains and the rivers exist! And as long as Rama's story has currency, so long shall you live in my realm.' (Sattar, chap. 2)

Thus, Valmiki is associated not simply with the content of the Ramayana but with its form as well. And with Brahma's blessing, he is responsible for his own immortality in Brahma's realm, which is specifically connected with the longevity of Rama's story on earth.

The orality of the tale is firmly established in its opening moments: Valmiki hears the story from Narada in response to his question. He is in a trance when Brahma appears to him and suggests that Valmiki tell this wondrous tale in the metre that he has just composed. We are not told whether Valmiki came out of his trance once Brahma left or whether he continued to be in his meditative state, 'seeing' the story of Rama unfold before his eyes as he recites it. But we are told that when he finished composing the long poem, including the Uttara Kanda,

> he began to wonder whom he would teach it to. As he was thinking about this, he was approached by two young bards wearing ascetics' clothes. These two young boys were glorious princes and were well versed in dharma. They were eloquent and had sweet voices and lived, at that time, with Valmiki in his hermitage.
>
> When Valmiki saw the two young boys who had faith in the Vedas, he decided to teach them his new poem. (Sattar, chap. 2)

The boys soon learn the poem and can recite it 'without a mistake'. They recite it for the sages and then make their way to Ayodhya where eventually they sing the entire poem for Rama at the sacrifice that he is conducting.

In the Uttara Kanda, Valmiki appears when Sita is banished into the forest after Rama hears market gossip about her. Under false pretences, Lakshmana takes her into the forest, and when he can be with her no longer, he tells her that he has brought her here to be abandoned on Rama's command. Trying to provide what solace he can, he tells her that the region is filled with the ashramas of kindly sages. 'The great sage Valmiki was a good friend of my father, Dasharatha. You can live comfortably by his feet, fasting and meditating' (Sattar, chap. 69). The children from Valmiki's hermitage find Sita alone and weeping. They tell Valmiki about her, but Valmiki already knows who she is through his second sight. He also knows that she is innocent and takes her into his fold, letting her live with the women ascetics who are part of his community. 'Even as you were coming here, I learned everything about you in the course of my meditation. In my heart, I know the reason for your arrival. My divine eye shows me that you are innocent. Have no fear, you can live with me' (Sattar, chap. 69). Sita's sons are born there and Valmiki names them Lava and Kusha.

Valmiki's climactic appearance in the Uttara Kanda gives rise to a truly astounding situation where Rama's sons sing the story of Rama's life to Rama in public. Everyone else gathered there remarks on their resemblance to Rama, who apparently cannot (or will not) recognize either his sons or his story until the part when the boys identify themselves as sons of Sita. This emotionally and narratively loaded recitation of the Ramayana within the Ramayana begins when Valmiki himself brings the boys to Ayodhya.

> As the sacrifice continued, the sage Valmiki came there with his students ... he said to Kusha and Lava, 'Go and sing to the brahmins, on the roads and the highways. Sing in the camps of kings. Sing at Rama's door, at the site of the rituals ... If the king should ask you whose sons you are, tell him only that you are Valmiki's students.' (Sattar, chap. 70)

When Kusha and Lava begin their recitation at the sacrifice, the company is enthralled by the poem and by the young bards' abilities.

> Eager to hear the rest of the poem, Rama asked the boys who shone with splendour, 'What is this poem about? Who composed it? Where does that great sage live?'
>
> 'It was composed by the blessed Valmiki who has come to attend your sacrifice. The poem tells the story of your life in great detail in five hundred cantos.' ... Rama listened to that lovely poem for many days in the company of kings, sages and monkeys. He learned from the poem that Kusha and Lava were the sons of Sita. In the midst of the assembly, Rama said, 'Go to the sage with this message. Tell him, "If Sita is really innocent and virtuous, let her come here with your permission and clear her name!" I would like to hear what the sage has to say on the matter.' (Sattar, chap. 70)

Valmiki acknowledges the royal summons. The next day,

> when Valmiki heard that everyone had arrived and that the crowd was still as a mountain, he hurried there with Sita ... Valmiki made his way through the throng with Sita and went up to Rama. 'This is the virtuous and righteous woman you abandoned in the forest near my hermitage even though she is innocent,' he said ... 'Her two sons, these wonderful bards, are your sons, Rama. I swear this is the truth! ... May I lose all the merit I have gained if Sita is not innocent! This blameless woman has never behaved inappropriately and thinks of her husband as a god. You were so scared of a little gossip! Now she will prove herself in front of you!' (Sattar, chap. 70)

Sita, instead of asking to stay with Rama if she is proven innocent, says, 'If I have never thought about any other man but Rama, let the goddess Madhavi create a chasm for me!' (Sattar, chap. 70). With that, Sita returns to the earth whence she came. After consoling Rama, the gods, who had arrived to witness Sita's second public trial of innocence, return to heaven,

> but the effulgent sages who lived there with [Brahma] took his permission and stayed behind on earth because they wanted to hear the rest of the poem.
>
> 'The sages from Brahma's realm are eager to hear what happens to me in the future,' said Rama to Valmiki. 'Start reciting that part from tomorrow.'

> Rama dismissed the gathering and, taking Kusha and Lava with him, he retired into the sacrificial enclosure. (Sattar, chap. 70)

The very last verse of the Uttara Kanda tells us that 'this story along with its supplement, the Uttara, was honoured by Brahma. It was created by Valmiki and is known as the Ramayana' (Sattar, chap. 71).

In both the Bala Kanda and the Uttara Kanda, Valmiki acts in the story he is telling, albeit in rather different ways. In the Bala Kanda, we know only that Valmiki decides to teach the two young bards who lived in his hermitage the wonderful story about the perfect man once he has found the new metre worthy of it.

> Rama happened to see the two young bards ... He took the boys, Kusha and Lava, with him to the palace ... he said to Lakshmana, Bharata and Shatrughna, 'Listen to this tale set in the new metre ... this is a unique and wonderful story' ... Encouraged by Rama's words, the boys sang softly, displaying their musical talents. And as Rama listened to them, he allowed himself to be drawn into the tale. (Sattar, chap. 2)

And thus, the wondrous tale of Rama and his ancestors begins in the opening book of the Sanskrit epic. Even here, where Valmiki plays a more passive role, he still becomes part of the story by virtue of his chance meeting with Rama's sons.

In the Uttara Kanda, the closing book of the Sanskrit epic, Valmiki intervenes more forcefully in the story as he deliberately sends Kusha and Lava to Rama's sacrifice with the explicit instructions that they must sing for Rama. As the Bala Kanda tells us that Valmiki knew more about Rama's story than is apparent to the rest of us through his meditative trance, the Uttara Kanda tells us that Valmiki had a divine eye. Thus, we can assume that, just as Valmiki knew about Sita's arrival in the forest and her innocence, he must know that Rama would at some point recognize his own story and ask to see Sita. He must also know that he himself will take Sita to the sacrifice and vouch for her innocence and that she will disappear into the earth. The disturbing remark from Rama that the gathered sages would like to hear what happened to him in the future and that Valmiki should continue with his story the next day makes more sense when we recall that when Brahma told Valmiki to tell Rama's story, he promised him that all that was unknown would be made known to him.

The first thing that needs to be examined is the nature of Valmiki's interventions in the story he tells: In one case, the Bala Kanda, he prepares the young bards to tell Rama's story. The chapters that set up this framed narrative moment do not overtly mention that the boys are Rama's sons, simply that they are two young men gifted with musical talent (the 'kushilavau') who live in Valmiki's hermitage. Here, the sage does not send the boys to Rama's sacrifice; Rama finds them singing their song and takes them along to his court so that they can repeat the same story for others. In the Uttara Kanda, not only does

Valmiki rescue Sita from her plight (having seen her innocence in his meditative trance), he knows who her sons are when he brings them up and teaches them the story of their father and their ancestors. He then tells them to take the story to their father. When Rama sends for him, Valmiki admonishes Rama for not trusting his wife. Not only does he declare Sita chaste, he also declares the boys to be Rama's sons.

In the Bala Kanda, it would seem that Valmiki comes out of his trance to teach the story to Kusha and Lava. Brahma instructs him to tell the story in the new metre and then disappears,

> but Valmiki and his disciples remained struck with wonder. The disciples repeated the new metre that had emerged from Valmiki's sorrow over and over again, and each time their delight and wonder increased. Then the great-souled sage announced, 'I will recite the history of Rama as a poem!' (Sattar, chap. 2)

We can assume that Valmiki has 'seen' the entire story during his trance, including his own part in it, and now proceeds to tell it more fully, embellished with poetry and rhetoric and completed by all the parts that were hitherto unknown. The complex and layered nature of authorial motivation here is even more strongly evident: the trance provides the story, the motivation to participate in the story, and the motivation to tell the story, all at the same time.

Since we have already met Kusha and Lava in the Bala Kanda as young boys, the Uttara Kanda is, technically, a flashback, as we are with Sita and Valmiki at a point in time before Kusha and

Lava are born. When Valmiki meets the abandoned Sita, the first thing he says to her is that his divine sight has told him who she is and that she is innocent. Was this 'divine sight' the meditative trance that he was in when Brahma appeared and promised him that the whole story of Rama would be made known to him? We must presume so, for Valmiki knows who Sita is when he meets her for the first time. Valmiki is, in fact, indirectly alluding both to his knowledge of the story and his motivations for telling it. He also knows what no one else can, the singular fact upon which *the* major incident of the Uttara Kanda is predicated: that during her captivity, Sita had remained true to her husband. The story that Narada told Valmiki about Rama ends with the return to Ayodhya and the happily-ever-after of the reclaimed throne and the prosperous reign that follows. But Valmiki's telling of Rama's story goes well beyond this point, as it must if he is to be the instrument of Rama's reunion with his legitimate heirs and the one who conclusively seals the debate about Sita's chastity. These two facts must be the things unknown that were made known to him as they remain, until the end, the two things that Rama does not know. In fact, Brahma specifically instructs Valmiki to 'recite the acts of Sita, the known ones and the unknown ones' (Sattar, chap. 2).

Furthermore, this meditative trance has implications for what the text makes known in the Bala Kanda to the multiple audiences for Rama's story. As we have seen, the Bala Kanda does not say that the two young boys whom Valmiki chooses as the bards for Rama's story are Rama's sons. But since Valmiki has been in his trance, he must know who they are and must know also that Rama would find them singing and take them to his court. Besides, if Valmiki knew who Sita was the moment he saw her (as we are told in the Uttara Kanda), he must also know that Rama's sons would be born to her in his hermitage. So, while Valmiki knows everything in the Bala Kanda itself, Rama and the rest of us, who are not part of a listening audience in the Bala Kanda, may not. Being among the listeners in the Bala Kanda, one can assume that Kusha and Lava find out who they are once they have learned the poem in its entirety, if they have not previously been told that in the course of their growing up. Just as Valmiki's modes of perceiving and acting in the story of Rama are simultaneous, so too, Kusha and Lava's modes of reciting and acting in the story of Rama are simultaneous.

Since orality and recitation are built into both the form and the content of the Indian epics, any listener or reader outside the tale being told becomes the external audience that receives the story through a successive series of quotation marks and reported speech. The first internal listeners in the Ramayana for the story of Rama are Valmiki himself and his disciples who hear it from Narada, who returns to heaven after he has narrated the tale. But the first listeners within the Ramayana for Valmiki's telling of Rama's story (that is, the Ramayana) are Lava and Kusha and the sage's other disciples. Kusha and Lava take Valmiki's version out into the world, to further and wider audiences. Their first public recitation is for sages and brahmins and, soon after, they are invited by Rama to recite the poem at his court. The tale becomes truly public at Rama's sacrifice where its audience includes kings and citizens, priests and commoners, jugglers, actors and musicians.[27]

---

[27] Both the Ramayana and the Mahabharata tell us that they are recited at sacrifices. Kings find out about their ancestors and about themselves in public.

And yet, there is an intriguing way in which Valmiki is also his own audience. If, indeed, Valmiki has seen all this in a meditative trance, where does he enter the story? Or is he 'always already present' inside it? David Shulman draws our attention to the intense narrative moment, which is practically epiphanic, in the Uttara Kanda when Rama moves from listening to his own story to experiencing it.

> The story is over. But the shocking and moving fact is that we experience these final chapters as Rama does – not in the backward movement of the story, but rather with the past become present or future (and the future presented as past). There is no visible seam separating the text's statement that Kusha and Lava sang the end of the poem from the actual content of the ending ... the frame has melted away, our sense of time is confused, past conflates with future – as it does already at the very beginning of the epic with Valmiki's proleptic vision of the past and future combined – and we find ourselves once again listening with Rama to the story of his own life, but at this point to that part of it which is still to unfold.[28]

This reflexive narrative moment is when the text is transformed into a Moebius strip. As Shulman says, the frame has imploded and the suddenly seamless narrative presents a single, continuous surface to its audience by turning into itself. What also happens at this moment is that the internal and external audiences for Rama's tale merge and become one. Shulman goes

---

[28] Cited in O'Flaherty (150–51).

on to say that we lose track, at this point, of who the narrator is: Is it Valmiki or is it his students, Rama's sons? And then he asks, 'Does it matter?'

For the purposes of this essay, which tries to locate Valmiki in the story he tells, it matters very much. I would argue that it is Valmiki who continues telling the story, and the reason is straightforward: once the cataclysmic moment with Sita has passed and the gods have returned to their realm, Rama takes his sons and leaves the sacrificial enclosure. But he has already told Valmiki that the sages want to hear more of the wondrous tale and has instructed him to continue telling it. The question here is not who is telling the story any more (for it is clear that it is Valmiki), but whether Rama is listening to his story as it unfolds or whether he is living it as Valmiki is telling it. Or whether Valmiki tells Rama's future in his absence, a future that Rama will live out in the course of time.

The questions about the seamless narrative moment are precisely these: Has Valmiki turned into an observer (like Sanjaya in the Mahabharata), who narrates what *is happening* as it happens to an audience that is (the sages and the monkeys) and is not (the external audience for the story) on the scene? Or is he telling Rama (and both the internal and external audiences) what *will happen* to Rama himself until the moment of his ascent to heaven? In either case, this moment, which Shulman lyrically describes as 'our sense of time [being] confused – past [conflating] with future', is, through Valmiki's proleptic vision, more than just a question of frame-breaking within the epic. The moment remains central to our potential understanding of where Valmiki (and Rama) might be in their stories at this point. Valmiki is, at this moment, most supremely his own audience, in that he is narrating either present or future events that he has already seen.

To put it another way, Valmiki already has the privilege of being inside and outside the epic – of seeing Rama's life unfold before his eyes from beginning to end (in a meditative trance or using his divine eye to see what he needs to see in order to tell it fully) and being a participant in that glorious tale. But we also have to consider the fact that Valmiki is seeing his own life flash before him and, therefore, seeing Rama's part in his life – that Valmiki is able to see (and tell) Rama's life only because a part of it is coincident with his own. Viewed from this somewhat inverted, but perhaps even more compelling, position, it is Rama, his wife and sons, who play a part in Valmiki's life (which the sage is privileged to see) and not the other way around. No doubt, within the universe of the Ramayana and its unequivocal opening question placed in Valmiki's mouth, for the gods and for the rest of us, it is Rama's life and deeds that are significant for the fate of the world (the restoration of dharma) and for humankind (the paradigm of the perfect man). We have to believe, then, that we all know Rama's story simply because Valmiki asked the question about the perfect man of Narada, that if he had not asked the question, the Ramayana (at least, if not other Rama stories) might have remained untold.

> Valmiki, the ascetic, questioned the eloquent Narada, bull among sages, always devoted to asceticism and the study of the sacred texts. 'Is there a man in the world today who is truly virtuous? Who is there who is mighty

> and yet knows both what is right and how to act upon it? Who always speaks the truth and holds firmly to his vows?' (Goldman, 121)

Narada answers the question relatively briefly, but we have to wait for the death of the krauncha bird, the creation of the new metre and Brahma's appearance in Valmiki's trance for the sage to retell the story that he heard from Narada. Moreover, it is (arguably) the promise from Brahma that Valmiki will know all that is unknown in the tale (presumably the parts that are either unknown or untold in the version that the sage heard from Narada) that elicits the retelling which becomes the Ramayana. Valmiki's trance and Brahma's reassuring and inspirational presence in the trance bring forth Rama's story from Valmiki and make it public, but this time, with Valmiki playing an active role in an epilogue of past and future narrative time, which did not occur in Narada's happily-ever-after end, with Rama's triumphal return to Ayodhya with his wife after the war. Narada's version of Rama's story states:

> Rama took Sita back but she was humiliated when he spoke to her harshly in front of all the people gathered there. Unable to bear the shame, that virtuous woman entered the fire. But as she entered the flames, flowers rained down from the sky and Agni declared her to be a chaste and honourable woman. (Sattar, chap. 1)

As a participant in the tale, Valmiki is absent within Narada's story of Rama's life and deeds; he is merely a listener. But in Valmiki's own tale, he becomes actor, teller and audience.

There is a grammatical point of interest relevant to this larger point in the text of the Bala Kanda: the Goldman translation of the first sarga shows the switch from the past (narrative) tense to the present tense after Rama has returned to Ayodhya. Towards the end of the first sarga, Goldman translates as follows:

> (69) He received boons from the gods and revived the fallen monkeys. Then mounting the flying chariot Pushpaka, he went to Nandigrama. (70) In Nandigrama the blameless man and his brothers put off the knotted hair of ascetics. Thus did Rama regain Sita and recover his kingdom. (71) His people are pleased and joyful, contented, well-fed and righteous. They are also free from physical and mental afflictions and the danger of famine.

The passage describing Rama's righteous reign continues in the present tense until the end of the sarga, which is the end of Narada's story. Further, in the Goldman translation, in sarga 3, after Valmiki has entered his trance and met Brahma who has urged him to tell Rama's story in the new metre, sarga 4 opens with: '(1) It was after Rama had regained his kingdom that the holy and self-controlled seer Valmiki composed this entire history in such wonderful words.'

Does Valmiki realize that Narada's tale is incomplete? Is it incomplete because Valmiki himself has not appeared in it to vouch for Sita's chastity and restore Rama's sons to him? Does the flip into the present tense in Narada's story (between what has happened and what is to happen, holding the future in its present-ness) so clearly displayed in the Goldman translation provide the point of entry for Valmiki's intervention in the story? The Goldman translation further suggests that Valmiki began his composition of Rama's life and deeds after Rama had regained his kingdom. Consonant with the larger point of this essay, we could take this to mean that the catalyst for Valmiki to retell Rama's story is his own role in it, articulated in the Bala Kanda and Uttara Kanda, both of which are located in a narrative time where Narada's story ends, after Rama's return to Ayodhya. It is the point at which Valmiki's and Rama's lives intersect that allows Valmiki to 'see' Rama's story.

The sage is privileged to see and tell the story of the perfect man because he has a crucial part to play in it. In addition, despite being his own audience in the story that he tells, Valmiki also adopts a third position – the position of the external audience, represented within the story itself by the market gossip about Sita's chastity. The gossip and gossipers (extra-textually, a washerman and his wife) express the suppressed question that *all* listeners, including the external audience, of the tale are dying to ask, since the main body of the story is silent about the period of time Sita spent in captivity and the length of time after which she becomes pregnant in Ayodhya. Valmiki enters and is able to answer the questions and complete the story (albeit tragically, despite his intervention) because he knows the parts unknown (Sita's unwavering fidelity and the legitimacy of Rama's sons) through his divine eye/meditative trance.

In his small book, *History at the End of the World,* Ranajit Guha compares ancient Indian modes of telling a narrative with Enlightenment modes. He argues that the moment of telling history that we find in the epics is conversational and experiential – that is, one tells history (or a story) because, in an encounter with another human being, one has been asked to tell it. A story is not based in an individual's sensory and empirical experience, but rather on the stock of known stories, called forth from the bard's memory by the needs of the audience. Valmiki cannot tell his tale without being part of the story, and the story cannot unfold of its own accord without Valmiki being in it. Thus, the author's tale is no simple narrative of imagination, nor even a simple narrative of experience. The Ramayana's author imagines himself telling the tale as part of the tale, and thereby predicts his own authorial experience. As author, audience and actor rolled into one, Valmiki creates an infinite reservoir of authorial motivation. And in this, he may have created a distinctly Indian form of authorship.

REMEMBERING IN THE RAMAYANA

THE PROBLEM OF MEMORY

Memory has been the leitmotif of this book: what Rama and Sita remember, how and when they remember it, and what consequence it has for their lives. I believe that the memories with the most serious consequences are Sita's memory of who Rama was before she was abducted and Rama's memory of his father's last act. Both these specific remembrances affect the way Rama and Sita eventually treat each other. Rama has to reject Sita at the end of the war because he does not want to be accused of having the same weakness as Dasharatha, that is, a love for a woman which was so overwhelming that it drove him to act against his dharma as a king. Sita is unable to recognize the man she meets at the end of the war, a man who has chosen his role as a warrior and a king, his public dharma, over the tender love he had shown her all her life – this choice makes it possible for her to leave him at the end of the story. Rama's memory has remained intact – he remembers the shame of Dasharatha's act as well as all the love he ever had for Sita. Sita's memory has proved more problematic – it cannot carry her past the reality of the man who has changed over their years of separation.

Perhaps the most powerful and poignant act of remembering is Rama's decision to create a golden statue of Sita in her absence. After Rama has banished Sita into the forest, he decides that he will perform the ashvamedha, the great horse sacrifice that will establish him as the king of kings. As he gives instructions for the preparations for the sacrifice, he says,

> 'Tell Bharata to go ahead with heaps of gold and silver. Let him go there with the traders, cooks, actors, dancers, brahmins, young and old people, and with carpenters and skilled workers, and mothers and sons, and all the residents of the inner apartments, as well as men skilled in the performance of these rites. Let him also take a golden statue of my wife.' (Sattar, chap. 70)

Rama does not want to forget what choosing to abide by his public dharma has led to. Nor does he want his people to forget what he has sacrificed for them. The statue of Sita serves as a public reminder not only of what Rama's kingship means, but also as a private reminder of what love might have been. Rama does not want to forget, he does not want time to heal his wound. He wants to live with his memory made present, as it were, presenting us with the wonderful paradox of the physical presence of an absence as well as a physical manifestation of the past in the present.

It is this manipulation of memory that allows Rama to retain his love for Sita, just as it is Sita's inability to manipulate her memory that causes her to forget (if not actually lose) her love for Rama. Sita's loss is doubly tragic for it was the memory of Rama and their time together that sustained her and her love for him during the long years of their separation, in the years of his physical absence from her. The reappearance of Rama in her life, the reality of his presence, destroys the memory she had and, along with that, destroys the love she had for Rama.

In the fragile universe of love in separation, how does memory construct, perhaps even constitute, love? Valmiki, in his Uttara Kanda, takes us to the brink of this chasm and leaves us there. He tells us that Rama was heartbroken and made a golden statue of Sita, but he tells us little about how Rama felt after she has gone. The statue of Sita is as much a symbol of her absence as it is a metaphor for his silence.

Nevertheless, while Valmiki takes us to the edge of Rama's desolation and goes no further, he does create the space for others to speculate on Rama's state of mind once Sita has left. Foremost among those who occupy this space, who take us deep into the chasm that separates love in the presence of and love in the absence of the beloved, is the twelfth-century Sanskrit playwright Bhavabhuti, whose masterful *Uttararamacharita* can be seen not simply as a response to Kalidasa's *Abhijnanashakuntalam* but also as an entirely fitting and deeply moving alternative to Rama's suppressed emotions and stoicism in Valmiki's Uttara Kanda.

In the Uttara Kanda, when Rama hears the marketplace gossip about Sita, he makes his terrible decision and he makes it alone. He calls his brothers to tell them what he needs to do and also that he shall brook no argument.

> Rama was told that the princes had arrived. Sadly, he hung his head and instructed the doorkeeper to let them in. The princes entered, wearing white clothes, their minds calm and composed. They saw that Rama's face was pale,

> like the moon in eclipse, or the sun dimmed at twilight. His eyes were filled with tears and his face was like a lotus shorn of all its glory. The princes touched his feet and waited for him to speak. (Sattar, chap. 69)

Surely this is an indication of Rama's anguish at the thought of forcing another separation from his beloved wife. As in the Yuddha Kanda, when Ravana has been killed and it is time for Rama to be reunited with Sita, what we see is his pain. Hanuman brings Rama a message from Sita, saying that she wants to see him. 'Rama was silent for a moment and his eyes filled with tears. He sighed and looked down at the ground' (Sattar, chap. 67). Even here, Rama knows that he has to test the woman he loves most, not because of his doubt about her behaviour, but because now he is the king and she has to be unimpeachable. His heart breaks as he prepares himself for the hardest moment in his life. In the Uttara Kanda, Rama goes on to say that he knows Sita is innocent but he cannot allow her to stay in the palace any longer.

> 'But now, the terrible things people are saying make me unhappy. An infamous man who is the subject of public discourse goes to the hells of the unrighteous and stays there as long as the story of his disgrace is told. The gods do not love the notorious and even the world loves a man who is well spoken of. Good men's deeds are motivated by a desire for fame. I would give up my life, even renounce all of you, for fear of a scandal. How can I hesitate or do anything less in Sita's case? So you see why I am so upset. I cannot imagine a greater sorrow than this!' (Sattar, chap. 69)

Later, when Rama summons Sita to the sacrifice and she calls upon the earth to take her away forever, Valmiki tells us,

> When the sacrifice was over, Rama was very depressed that Sita was no longer with him. The entire world seemed empty to him and, overcome by his grief, he knew no peace of mind. He rewarded the brahmins and sent them away along with the kings, the rakshasas and the monkeys. When they had all left, he went back to Ayodhya, carrying Sita in his heart.
>
> He did not marry again, and for every sacrifice after that, he placed a golden statue of Sita by his side. (Sattar, chap. 70)

How different are these controlled emotions, this silent heartbreak, compared to the moment in the forest when Rama realizes that Sita has been abducted! There, his grief is wildly and loudly manifest – he runs from tree to tree, from the mountains to the river, begging the flowers, the birds, the animals for news of his beloved. It is almost as if the mature Rama, the man who returns to be king, has left his capacity to feel so intensely behind in the forest.

In Valmiki's Ramayana, there are only three occasions when we are privy to Rama's innermost thoughts and to his pain. The first time we see Rama vulnerable is in the very early moments of his exile, when he weeps not only at having left his ailing father and disconsolate mother, but also at his own misfortune. After this, Rama's equanimity is destroyed only in relation to Sita – witness his complete loss of control when he realizes that Sita has been taken away from him after he has killed the magic deer. When Rama returns and finds the little hut empty, he runs through the forest in search of her. He cries out,

> 'O kadamba tree, have you seen my beloved who loved your fruit so? Tell me if you know where that lovely woman is! Bilva tree, where is she, the woman whose breasts are like your fruit, who is as delicate as the new shoots in her yellow silks? O palm tree, take pity on me and tell me if you have seen that beautiful woman. Rose-apple tree, my beloved's complexion has the hues of your fruit. You must have seen her. Tell me where she is!
>
> 'Little deer, you must know where the doe-eyed Sita is! Is she with you in the forest? O best of elephants, Sita had thighs like your trunk, you must know where she is!' (Sattar, chap. 34)

Rama likens Sita to the trees and the flowers and the animals. In his distress, everything around him reminds him of her – the eyes of a doe, the colour of a fruit, the trunk of an elephant. Through these comparisons, he is conjuring up his beloved, hair by hair, limb by limb. In her profound and complete absence, he is invoking her presence. In doing so, he is remembering her in all her sensuous physicality – her breasts, her lips, her thighs.

Later still, when the rains have ended and it appears that Sugriva is in no hurry to make good his promise to begin the search for Sita, Rama gives vent to a raging anger that unnerves even Lakshmana, who has to calm him down. As he sits alone during the rainy season, Rama thinks again of his absent beloved. He says to Lakshmana,

> 'The earth parched by the summer heat and now flooded with water reminds me of Sita shedding tears after being scorched by her grief ... And the lightning flashing across the dark clouds makes me think of Sita writhing in Ravana's dark arms! Look at the flowers on the hillside, Lakshmana! They rejoice in the fresh rainwater and make me think of love! ... Sleep comes as slowly as a river moving to the ocean, but the crane rushes to the cloud and the woman runs to her lover.' (Sattar, chap. 39)

When the skies clear at the end of the rains, Rama's grief does not abate.

> He gazed in anguish at the clear sky and the white orb of the moon ... sitting on top of that mountain streaked with metallic ores, his thoughts turned to Sita.
>
> 'Ah my beloved! Her voice was as sweet as a bird's! How can she rejoice in birdsong now, as she used to in our forest hut? How can she enjoy these golden flowering bushes like she used to when I was by her side? How must she feel now when she hears birds calling to their mates? I feel no joy in wandering through the woods with their streams and pools without doe-eyed Sita by my side!' cried Rama, lord of all men, lamenting like the chataka bird begging the gods for water. (Sattar, chap. 39)

Similarly, when Sita is in captivity and sets her mind upon Rama to get her through those desperate and lonely days and nights, it is her memories that she calls upon, the intimate memories of the idyllic time they spent together in the forest. We are unexpectedly allowed to share their intimacy when Hanuman arrives in the ashoka grove and Sita gives him a story to take back to Rama, a story that only he knows, a story that will prove that she is Sita and that Hanuman has found the right woman. Saying, 'the best token that I can give you is this message' (Sattar, chap. 50), she tells the monkey of the time when a crow pecked her breast and Rama was so angry that he empowered an insignificant blade of kusha grass to chase the crow through the three worlds and destroy him. Though she is speaking to Hanuman, Sita addresses the story to Rama.

> 'One day, when my body was still wet from my bath, you fell asleep with your head in my lap. A crow carrying a piece of meat in his beak began to attack me ... I was angry with the bird and drew off my girdle. But my clothes slipped off and, at that moment, you awoke and saw me. You began to laugh and I was terribly embarrassed. I hid in your arms to get away from the crow ... You wiped the tears from my eyes and my face and, hissing like an angry serpent, you said, "Lady with thighs like an elephant's trunk, who has dared to strike you on the breast?"' (Sattar, chap. 50)

Sita's story has two aspects to it: one, that she, too, invokes Rama's presence by recalling a deeply private and sensual memory, and two, that she uses this intimate story not simply as a token of recognition that she sends through Hanuman, but as a trigger for Rama to remember her as fully as possible, to remember her in body as much as in spirit.

The Sanskrit word 'abhijnana' applies both to the object that triggers memory (the memento) and to the act of remembering (the moment of recognition). And it is precisely this ambivalence, this bi-valence, that Kalidasa calls upon in his *Abhijnanashakuntalam*. For the story that Kalidasa chooses to tell about Shakuntala, the daughter of Menaka and Vishvamitra, and Dushyanta the king, is one of forgetting, of the erasure of memory and the consequent complete absence of love. In Kalidasa's nataka (bound as it is by generic conventions but no less moving for that), Dushyanta is not a rake. He intends to remain true to his forest maiden, his innocent Shakuntala of the hermitage, but a curse wipes out his memory, a memory not only of the promise he made to her, but of their love itself. The restoration of love is bound up with a token of that love and that promise, in this case, a ring.

What is fascinating about the curse that Kalidasa creates for his play is how dislocated it is. The sage Durvasa curses Shakuntala because she is too distracted to greet him – he says that whoever she is thinking of will forget her. The object of the curse is Dushyanta, even though the weight of the curse falls upon Shakuntala. It is Shakuntala who suffers because she cannot forget her love, but Dushyanta has no memory of the love that he has lost and so, is free of the suffering that the curse bestows.[29]

[29] Shakuntala is not aware of the curse that is about to increase her misfortunes. And, as the audience of the play, since we only hear about the curse later, we, too, are distanced from Shakuntala and her suffering.

Like Sita, Shakuntala faces ignominy and shame through her husband's public rejection of her. In Kalidasa's play, when Shakuntala arrives, pregnant, at Dushyanta's court, the curse is active and he does not remember her. Additionally, the ring he gave her, which was to be the abhijnanam, the token of recognition as well as the symbol of his promise and the public acknowledgement of their relationship, has fallen off her finger. By the time the ring is found and Dushyanta retrieves his memory, Shakuntala and his son are far away – she has returned to the celestial realm of her mother. In the nataka, the curse expires when the memento appears and so, the memory of love comes flooding back, as fresh and rich as ever. Once his memory returns, Dushyanta suffers great torment in the absence of his beloved. But after some grieving years alone, Dushyanta is reunited with his family and recovers the love that he had lost, both emotionally and physically.

In a similar (but more devastating) separation, Sita has returned to her mother despite the fact that Rama has proved in front of his own people that her conduct has been unimpeachable. Rama now has his sons, but he continues to suffer: his 'curse' is that he cannot forget, that he has never forgotten, his memory remains frozen, immaculate. He banished Sita into the forest not because he had forgotten his love for her but because he had suppressed it.

What is interesting in Kalidasa's emotion-drenched, romantic universe is that Dushyanta, unlike Rama, suffers from the imperfection, the incompleteness of his erased memory. Although he has forgotten Shakuntala, there is a trace of memory, a 'vasana', that lurks at the fringes of his consciousness, reminding him that he has forgotten something precious. The shadow disturbs him and he feels cut off from his own past. Rama, on the other hand, remains desolately rooted in his past, symbolized by the golden statue of his absent wife.

Memory in Bhavabhuti's *Uttararamacharita* becomes more than the dramatic device it is in Kalidasa's *Abhijnanashakuntalam*. Here, it is practically a state of being for Rama and for Sita. Bhavabhuti's layering of past and present, of memory and reality, continues throughout the play in dizzying swirls of psychological time and real space. Leaving no stone of reflexivity unturned, he even includes a play within his play where a Valmiki restores Sita to a grieving Rama. In both plays, Bhavabhuti's as well as Valmiki's, there is a happy ending, a reunion after all those terrible years apart. There can be a happy ending precisely because of the perfection, the completeness of both Rama's and Sita's memories, for their love was never erased through forgetting. Rather, it has been restored, if not newly and more fully constituted, through acts of memory.

Bhavabhuti places memory front and centre as his play opens. Rama and Sita are at an exhibition of paintings that depict moments from their life together. Both of them recall how happy they were in the forest, Sita remarking that she feels almost as if she were reliving those gentle times, as if the past were present. Rama remembers even the anguish he felt when Sita was taken from him, which is a wonderful memory of a memory of love and pain. Sita is disturbed by the pictures from Janasthana because they make her remember that she was separated from her beloved Rama soon after. She falls asleep and, as she dreams about their (past) separation and calls out in anguish in her sleep, Durmukha arrives with news of the market gossip about her. Just before Rama resolves that she must be sent away, starting, as such, their later and more heartbreaking separation, he says,

> She is Lakshmi herself living
> in my house, ambrosial balm
> for my eyes, the touch of rich sandalwood cream upon
>   my body;
> this arm of hers around my neck
> is a cool and smooth pearl necklace.
> What don't I love about her – except
> the torture of being apart.
> (Pollock, 109)

After Rama has killed Shambuka, he returns to Panchavati where the forest deities allow Sita a glimpse of him. She can see him, wracked as he is by memories of their time in the idyllic forest glades, but he cannot see her. She touches him and her hand brings back a flood of memories. Rama says,

> Surely I am familiar with this
> from long ago, this touch
> that both restores my consciousness and induces a
>   deep delirium:
> no sooner does it dispel the faintness
> that arises from my anguish than it produces the
>   stupefaction of an absolute bliss.
> (Pollock, 183)

A truly amazing scene follows, where Rama and Sita speak to each other but not to each other, each addressing a surrogate, each remembering love with a profound sense of longing and loss. More importantly, each is conjuring up the other as a real being, capable even of being touched and felt.

As we have seen in Kalidasa, memory needs a trigger – whether it is a signet ring or a song. In the *Uttararamacharita* too, memory is not spontaneous, there is an external object that commands it. In the opening scene of the play, it is the picture exhibition that stimulates such strong memories that Rama and Sita are practically transported back in time and space to the forest. This same scene also introduces another abhijnanam, the magical jrimbhaka weapons by which Rama will eventually recognize his sons. This abhijnanam is not about memory, it is about finding something new that somehow always belonged to you. When Kalidasa's Dushyanta is finally reunited with his family, his fatherhood of the precocious little boy he sees is confirmed by the fact that he can touch the charm that the boy wears around his neck.

In Valmiki's Ramayana, Sita sends Hanuman back with not only her last remaining jewel but also with a story, so that Rama might remember how he loved her and come to rescue her all the sooner. The story as much as the jewel is the abhijnanam, the trigger for Rama's memory of how they have loved each other. The story as a device that retrieves memory and, in doing so, affirms identity is used often in the Valmiki Ramayana. The most exciting of these instances is when Jambavan 'reminds' Hanuman who he is by telling him the story of his birth at a time when all seems lost and the monkeys are in despair on the shores of the mighty ocean.

> [Jambavan] set about trying to urge the heroic Hanuman, the very best of all the monkeys, who was sitting happily by himself ... 'Hero among monkeys, so learned in all the traditional texts, you sit alone and in silence ... strength, intelligence, splendour and a commitment to truth make you special among all beings. Awake to yourself!' (Sattar, chap. 44)

And once Hanuman is told who he is and realizes the great boons that have been bestowed on him, he expands, literally and metaphorically, and becomes equal to the task that lies ahead of him.

In much the same way, Rama needs to be told his own story over and over again for him to remember who he is. When the gods return Sita to him after she has walked into the fire, they say,

> 'You are the creator of the worlds and the foremost of the wise! How could you let Sita walk into the fire? Don't you know that you are the greatest among the gods?' ... Rama, the lord of the worlds, the best among those who practise dharma, said, 'I always thought I was human, that I was Rama, the son of Dasharatha. Tell me who I am. Where did I come from? Why am I here?' (Sattar, chap. 67)

Strictly speaking, at this juncture, the gods don't tell Rama the story of his life, they simply tell him who he is. The story of

Rama's life is told to Rama in the most dramatic of all possible ways – his estranged sons recite his story to him at the sacrifice he is conducting. Here, the story is the abhijnanam that functions in a number of different ways, as the token that triggers memory and the act of recognition, simultaneously. For Rama, once he recognizes himself in the story, it reminds him how he has lived his life and lost his great love. It also allows him to 'recognize' and acknowledge his sons in public.

After hearing the first twenty cantos, 'eager to hear the rest of the poem, Rama asked the boys who shone with splendour, "What is this poem about? Who composed it? Where does that great sage live?"' (Sattar, chap. 70). Obviously, Rama has been listening to the beginning of the story that talks about how the Ramayana was composed. The boys respond to his question by saying, 'It was composed by the blessed Valmiki who has come to attend your sacrifice. The poem tells the story of your life in great detail in five hundred cantos' (Sattar, chap. 70).

Rama either realizes or acknowledges that he is listening to his own story at a crucial juncture in the boys' narrative.

> Rama listened to that lovely poem for many days in the company of the kings, sages and monkeys. He learned from the poem that Kusha and Lava were the sons of Sita. In the midst of the assembly, Rama said, 'Go to the sage with this message. Tell him, "If Sita is really innocent and virtuous, let her come here with your permission and clear her name!" I would like to hear what the sage has to say on this matter.' (Sattar, chap. 70)

When the story being told to him reaches the point where he banishes Sita, Rama's love for Sita comes flooding back and he becomes painfully aware that he is (still) separated from her. The past and the present telescopically collapse into each other through the pain that Rama remembers and the pain that he is feeling now, as if the memory and the reality were one. Bhavabhuti crystallizes this narrative conceit (the simultaneity of the remembered pain and the felt pain) and produces a multifaceted and highly polished dramatic gem from it. In Bhavabhuti's play, Valmiki is a playwright who brings to Rama the moment of Rama's separation from Sita in a play within the play, even as he carries the story ahead of what has actually happened to Rama at that point. In Bhavabhuti's play, Rama has sent Sita into the forest and continues to perform his royal duties despite his crushing sadness. In the fictional Valmiki's play that Bhavabhuti's Rama is watching, Sita begs her mother, the earth, to take her away after she has given birth to her sons. As Rama swoons in grief, unable to bear even the artifice of a further and more permanent separation from Sita, Valmiki the playwright reveals himself to also be Sita's protector in her abandonment and restores her to Rama.

Bhavabhuti's play must have the happy ending, the all-is-forgiven reunion, that its genre, the nataka, dictates. By the same generic measure, one could argue that Valmiki's epic is about kingship and lineage and authority and so, what happens to Sita is far less important than the fact of Rama's union with his sons. It is not Rama and Sita's love that carries the narrative thread, it is the legitimacy of Rama's heirs. But Valmiki is too sensitive to leave our questions about Rama dangling, especially since he has already used memory as such a powerful device of evocation in his work. With Sita's exit, Valmiki's tale has lost its emotional centre. This becomes a hollow space that can only be filled with another emotion, that is, Rama's memory of happier times. As Valmiki maintains the integrity and courage of his chaste heroine by allowing Sita to reject Rama at the end of her story, he is equally uncompromising about Rama's anguished loneliness as his story continues. Did Valmiki compose a story about a man/god who could do no wrong? How so, if in the end it is this same man/god who has been left devastated? Might we imagine that, in the end, Valmiki has shown his hand and told us whose side he is on? I would like to think so.

BIBLIOGRAPHY

Erndl, Kathleen M. 1992. 'The Mutilation of Surpanakha'. In *Many Ramayanas: The Diversity of a Narrative Tradition in South Asia*, ed. Paula Richman, 67–88. New Delhi: Oxford University Press.

Goldman, Robert P., trans. 1984. *Balakanda*. Vol. 1 of *The Ramayana of Valmiki*. Princeton: Princeton University Press.

Guha, Ranajit. 2002. *History at the End of the World*. New York: Columbia University Press.

O'Flaherty, Wendy Doniger. 1988. *Other People's Myths: The Cave of Echoes*. New York: Macmillan.

Patton, Laurie, and David Haberman, eds. 2010. *Notes from a Mandala*. Newark: University of Delaware Press.

Pollock, Sheldon, trans. 2007. *Rama's Last Act by Bhavabhuti*. New York: New York University Press JJC Foundation.

Ramanujan, A.K. 1992. 'Three Hundred Ramayanas: Five Examples and Three Thoughts on Translation'. In *Many Ramayanas: The Diversity of a Narrative Tradition in South Asia,* ed. Paula Richman, 22–49. New Delhi: Oxford University Press.

Sattar, Arshia, trans. 2019. *Valmiki's Ramayana*. New Delhi: HarperCollins India.

Shulman, David. 1992. 'Fire and Flood: The Testing of Sita in Kampan's *Iramavataram*'. In *Many Ramayanas: The Diversity of a Narrative Tradition in South Asia,* ed. Paula Richman, 89–113. New Delhi: Oxford University Press.

CROSS-EDITION REFERENCE

For Arshia Sattar's Translation of the Valmiki Ramayana

HarperCollins India (2019) and Rowman & Littlefield (2018) Editions	Penguin Classics (2000) Edition
Childhood	***Childhood***
Chapter 1	Chapter 1
Chapter 2	Chapter 2
Chapter 3	Chapter 3
Chapter 4	Chapter 4
Chapter 5	Chapter 5
Chapter 6	Chapter 6
Chapter 7	Chapter 7
Chapter 8	Chapter 8
Chapter 9	Chapter 9
Chapter 10	Chapter 10
Chapter 11	Chapter 11
Chapter 12	Chapter 12

HarperCollins India and Rowman & Littlefield Editions	Penguin Classics Edition
Ayodhya	***Ayodhyā***
Chapter 13	Chapter 1
Chapter 14	Chapter 2
Chapter 15	Chapter 3
Chapter 16	Chapter 4
Chapter 17	Chapter 5
Chapter 18	Chapter 6
Chapter 19	Chapter 7
Chapter 20	Chapter 8
Chapter 21	Chapter 9
Chapter 22	Chapter 10
Chapter 23	Chapter 11
Chapter 24	Chapter 12
Chapter 25	Chapter 13
Chapter 26	Chapter 14
Chapter 27	Chapter 15
Wilderness	***Wilderness***
Chapter 28	Chapter 1
Chapter 29	Chapter 2
Chapter 30	Chapter 3
Chapter 31	Chapter 4
Chapter 32	Chapter 5
Chapter 33	Chapter 6
Chapter 34	Chapter 7

HarperCollins India and Rowman & Littlefield Editions	Penguin Classics Edition
Kishkindha	***Kiṣkindha***
Chapter 35	Chapter 1
Chapter 36	Chapter 2
Chapter 37	Chapter 3
Chapter 38	Chapter 4
Chapter 39	Chapter 5
Chapter 40	Chapter 6
Chapter 41	Chapter 7
Chapter 42	Chapter 7 (ch. no. repeated)
Chapter 43	Chapter 8
Chapter 44	Chapter 9
Beauty	***Beauty***
Chapter 45	Chapter 1
Chapter 46	Chapter 2
Chapter 47	Chapter 3
Chapter 48	Chapter 4
Chapter 49	Chapter 5
Chapter 50	Chapter 6
Chapter 51	Chapter 7
Chapter 52	Chapter 8
Chapter 53	Chapter 9
Chapter 54	Chapter 10

HarperCollins India and Rowman & Littlefield Editions	Penguin Classics Edition
War	***War***
Chapter 55	Chapter 1
Chapter 56	Chapter 2
Chapter 57	Chapter 3
Chapter 58	Chapter 4
Chapter 59	Chapter 5
Chapter 60	Chapter 6
Chapter 61	Chapter 7
Chapter 62	Chapter 8
Chapter 63	Chapter 9
Chapter 64	Chapter 10
Chapter 65	Chapter 11
Chapter 66	Chapter 12
Chapter 67	Chapter 13
Chapter 68	Chapter 14
Epilogue	***Epilogue***
Chapter 69	Chapter 1
Chapter 70	Chapter 2
Chapter 71	Chapter 3

INDEX

ACKNOWLEDGEMENTS

This book has been on my mind for several years, both consciously and unconsciously. I know that some of what it contains has been learned and heard from people whom I remember (who are mentioned here) and there is equally much from people whom I have forgotten. It has emerged from years of obsessive conversations, monologues rather, on my part, and patient listening and sparkling insights from those who were subjected to them. It represents, in many ways, the culmination of one part of my relationship with this magnificent text, a relationship that has not been easy or smooth. I have struggled through the Sanskrit, first for my dissertation and then for the published translation, I have been stunned by the beauty of its images and been frustrated by its seeming coldness. I have fought Rama in my heart and mind, I have wept for all that Sita has lost and been impatient with her for enduring all that she did without a murmur. I have felt Ravana's awesome power, I have flown through the magical skies with Hanuman and I have shared the intoxication of the monkeys in Madhuvana. I have heard Valmiki's voice in my dreams and I have tried not to shout him down, especially when I disagreed. Not all of these moments are represented in these essays but they constitute the landscape against which they were conceived and written.

The essays have had many sympathetic readers in the years that it took to write them: Malika Anand, Vinay Jawahar, Lakshmi Holmström, Rachel Saltz and Raghu Karnad. All provided encouragement, made suggestions and detailed comments, and helped me clean up the writing and the ideas. Vinod Ravindran shared the giddy exhilaration of a 'damn good idea'. Students of the Earlham College's South Asia Study Abroad Program since 2005 have been subjected to early and later iterations of the ideas in the book, so also, students at the National Institute of Design, the Film and Television Institute of India, and students in the University of Chicago's South Asia Study Abroad Program – teaching the text and having the opportunity to try out some of the more contentious ideas in the book has been invaluable in helping me clarify my thoughts and in sifting through the various reactions to the interpretations I offer. I thank the people who made this teaching possible: Rajaram Krishna, Shilpa Das, Anjum Rajabali and Mark Lycett. Laurie Patton helped me with the knotty problems of the chapter on Valmiki and I know that the chapter would have been less without her questions and suggestions. Wendy Doniger is 'always already' in everything that I write – without all that she has taught me and given me over the last twenty-five years and her timely interventions, none of this would be possible. A.K. Ramanujan also lives in this book as he does in all the ways that I have learned to read the Indian epics.

The germ of this book emerged from a casual conversation with Girish Karnad – I thank him for pushing me to write again. Time to read and write and think through this project was generously provided by fellowships at the Ledig House writers' residency in the summer of 2007 and at the Rockefeller Foundation's Bellagio Centre in 2009. Friends who were gentle but firm in their support while I was in residence at Ledig include Nayana Currimbhoy, Bronwen Bledsoe, Rachel Saltz and N.S. Köenings. Thoughtful comments from Pilar Palaciá, Christine Lucia and Mariko Nagai in Bellagio made me think anew about what I have said and why I have said it the way I have. The book has also benefited from conversations with performers and visitors at Adishakti in the course of their Ramayana project, most especially David Shulman who continues to urge us all forward in our work with his sustained lyricism and his critical insights. I thank Veenapani Chawla for inviting me to participate in the first year of that project. Also for the Adishakti programme, Rustom Bharucha urged me to look at Bhavabhuti and I thank him for persistent encouragement with the text and a sustained conversation on aesthetics. R. Sivapriya, my editor for this book, helped me through some seriously tangled underbrush. I am immensely grateful for the clarity of her thoughts and for her flexibility on so many fronts.

For love and warmth and food and drink, Shai, Arati and Shetty, Fizz, Pascal and Elsa, Rachel, Bronwen, Suzan and Fahim, Malika and Vinay, Trupti and Ravi; for the unique sustenance of witching and magic, Nayana and Raisa; for patience and infinite grace, my mother Nazura; and for all that makes my life so lush, Sanjay, to whom this book is dedicated.

ABOUT THE AUTHOR

Arshia Sattar holds a PhD in South Asian Languages and Civilizations from the University of Chicago. She teaches classical Indian literature at several institutions in India, and writes for a number of journals and magazines.